T0103835

# ONE MINUTE DUBAI

# ONE MINUTE DUBAI

---

A Man's Journey Towards Success

Arthur Kuizon

PARTRIDGE

| ISBN: | Softcover | 978-1-4828-5478-7 |
| --- | --- | --- |
| | eBook | 978-1-4828-5482-4 |



Print information available on the last page.

**To order additional copies of this book, contact**
Toll Free 800 101 2657 (Singapore)
Toll Free 1 800 81 7340 (Malaysia)
orders.singapore@partridgepublishing.com

www.partridgepublishing.com/singapore

# DEDICATION

This book is dedicated to all hardworking expatriates not only in Dubai U.A.E but in the whole world who left their homeland and sacrifice everything in the hope that they would find the journey to success. Frequent travellers/visitors will also benefit in reading this book because it is informative and contains general facts and reminders about Dubai, U.A.E.

All glory to God, our creator, provider and protector.

## A Time for Everything

What do we gain from all our work? I know the heavy burdens that God has laid on us. He has set the right time for everything. He has given us desire to know the future, but never gives us the satisfaction of fully understanding what He does. So I realized that all we can do is be happy and do the best while we are still alive.

Ecclesiastes 3:9-12

## A Door of Opportunity

I know your deeds. See, I have placed before you a door that no one can shut. I know that you have little strength, yet you have kept my word and have not denied my name.

Revelation 3:8

# ONE MINUTE

I have only just a minute
Only sixty seconds in it,
Forced upon me,
can't refuse it.
Didn't seek it,
didn't choose it,
But it's up to me to use it.
I must suffer if I lose it,
give account if I abuse it.
It is only just a minute,
But eternity is in it.

- Anonymous

# Contents

# MISSION-VISION

The mission of the One Minute Dubai is to give its readers one minute view of Dubai at every end of its chapter, and the great opportunities that awaits them. And it is the wish of the author to give you a practical guide on how to become successful in Dubai whether you are here for pleasure, business or to work.

The author has interviewed people coming from all over the globe who lives, works and stay in Dubai, coming from different perspective – tourist, expats, businessmen, students, locals, etc.

You'll find out why more and more people are falling in love with one of the fastest growing city in the world; It is where the East meets the West.

This book will serve as your key and gateway to Dubai – If Dubai is a journey to your success, then this book is your map, light and compasses to reach it.

# WHY ONE MINUTE DUBAI?

Among a dozen of book that has been written about Dubai, OMD is a novel based on the actual encounters, stories and experiences of people in Dubai. Thus, it's not only a general info book but it's also a self help book written in a novelty that no has done before.

If you want to share your own story of success you may register at www.successfulpinoyako.com and email it to admin@ successfulpinoyako.com and a special gift awaits for those stories that will be chosen.

# FOREWORD

In today's modern world, leading cities like Dubai needs high demand professionals in various fields and industries and Filipinos in particular are very much in demand not only because of their professional qualification and experience but they also have the TLC ( tender,loving,care) factor.

Migration is by choice and it comes with great sacrifice, pain and toil. But given the right preparation and perspective it will also result into great success and achievement in life.

The author has opened the mind and eyes of expat professionals that migration is not an automatic success if you don't have the proper guidance and perspective just like what happened in the story. You will see and feel it for yourself that events are unfolding

As an envoy of my people and my country it my duty and obligation I have to ensure that all are given the right path and opportunity to become successful especially when one decided to go back home. In fact we have started a drive for financial literacy program called PINOYWISE.

I highly recommend this book for all of those who want to try their destiny abroad.

Ambassador Grace Princesa
Philippine Ambassador to the U.A.E.

# INTRODUCTION

Transformation and Progress of Dubai

Since the oil exploration in the 1950's and its discovery in the late 60's, Dubai has truly emerged, transformed and evolved. From small fishing community and Pearl Industry, Dubai has become not only as a tourist destination but a global hub for business, trade, media, I.T., aviation and financial services; thanks to the visionary leadership of HH Shiekh Mohammed bin Rashid Al Maktoum, VP of UAE and ruler of Dubai. No doubt, Dubai has been put in the global map.

An excerpt from the book; My Vision – Challenges in the Race for Excellence by HH Shiekh Mohammed bin Rashid Al Maktoum:

> ***"The UAE experience represents a role model for what a country can achieve when it is blessed by a leadership that cares about people and works in the interest of the whole community. Credibility in this drive is achieved by actions not sayings. This makes the big difference between a leadership that considers people as the real wealth of the nation and another that considers them as the real burden.***

> ***To overcome challenges of a new century in a new millennium, we need a way of thinking and innovative approaches that help us achieve social developments and accelerates the development process. We need to change our thinking patterns, to be able to understand the world's language, to convey our mission and stances clearly and simply so that the whole can understand us. This will deepen cooperation and eliminate misunderstanding among nations and will give the chance to direct all efforts towards development".***

By reading One Minute Dubai you will have an in-depth knowledge about Dubai and apply it to your own life.

This book is for you, who aspire to be successful in Dubai, or even in life. It will truly uplift your heart and soul.

Enjoy reading. It is the ultimate wish of the author that you may find the road to your success.

# ACKNOWLEDGEMENT

As the popular saying goes that there are three ways to leave a legacy on earth: to plant a tree; bear a child; and write a book. Well, I guess the first two is pretty much easy. I mean, when I was a kid at school I could still remember that we were asked to plant a bean seed ( I don't know where is it now...). For the second thing, to bear or have a child, I didn't have any trouble on this as I became a proud father on my early adult life. But for the last one, to write a book, I can say is a pretty tough one. As not anyone can write a book. For I know a lot of people and friends who wanted to write one but they really never started to put in into action.

It took me almost 4 years to finish this book project. It all started as an idea on January 2011. And the late nights and sometimes sleepless nights started in order to put all the story into writing. But all the pain, hardship and effort were not in vain.

I am very privilege and honoured to write this book all for the glory and kingdom of the God Almighty. For He was the on who showed me the wisdom and understanding on this project.

I would like to personally give thanks to my mentor Ximo Ramos for all the mentoring and support. For my One Minute Group namely: Andre, Jake, Nesty, Paolo and Mary (where where you all this time?). You guys are all amazing!

To my African Brethren- Indeed, our fellowship every Tuesday, Thursday and Saturday were not in vain for the Lord revealed to me His greater plan through our fellowship. You folks are very humble and powerful. And of course to my Mom in Faith Sister Mercy, may the Almighty God continue to anoint you and favour you. I have seen in my own eyes the hand of God touching and changing the lives of people in our ministry.

To all of my friends and colleagues who supported me in this project ( the list is so long) you know who you are. I want to thank you all. To My SuccessfulPinoyAko group,my Sega Family, my Taco Bell friends, my short but fruitful stay in Mercedes Benz and to my manager who told me that she no longer needed me in her team and I can leave my desk and never show up – I just wanted to say - I really wanted to thank you for everything, for the opportunity you have given me. You have inspired me…

And to all of my detractors and enemies I just want to bless you all and I pray that you may also find your purpose in life.

# The Departure

*"A journey of a thousand miles begins with a single step."*

*Lao-tzu Chinese philosopher*
*(604 BC - 531 BC)*

Its 6' o clock in the morning and the alarm started ringing. For Robert, it's probably the hardest thing he'll ever do in his life – to wake up, get dressed, carry his luggage and leave his wife Jenny, and his 1 year-old son Ash, while they are still sleeping.

Robert decided to go at the airport alone for he's afraid that he may changed his mind if he sees his wife and son saying goodbye.

"If I could only stop the ticking of the clock,", he whispered. Every minute, even second is a precious moment for Robert, spending his last moment with them at least for the next several years.

A glimpse of Ash right after he was being born suddenly appeared in his memory:

*"Jenny, now that were blessed with a son. I'll do everything to give you the best in the world".*

> *"Even it means leaving us Robert? I told you that you don't have to leave we're contended with what we have. But if you really have to go then I will give my full support even if it will break my heart"...*

As he gently kisses his wife and son, he left a note, put it under his wife's pillow. As he wrote:

> "To my Loving Wife,
>
> Thank you honey for all the love, support and care you have given to me and to our son. There is nothing more I can ask for... But I have to do this, and leave you for the meantime because I love you and our son so much and I want to give the best of the world to both of you. Remember those days when we use to dream under the stars, and we always look for the falling star to make a wish. The laughter and tears we used to share. Though empty-handed yet we're full of joy and hope. Such sweet to reminisce. And now we've been blessed by a child
>
> Maybe I'll be gone for a while but my heart will always be with you. As soon as you wake up I might be gone but I'll be back... soon. And she glances on the window and view the 3 kings star in the heaven (as they always do when they day dream).
>
> Love,
> Robert

As soon as Robert was about to leave the gate, a loud voice called him. "Robert promise me you'll be back for us and we will be waiting for you".

> *Throughout my career as a cab driver I've seen a lot of successful people who made it in abroad and achieve their dreams. Although some folks come home empty-handed.*

Jennifer said while she carries their son. And Robert hugged her very tight and whispered to her ears: "I promise that I'll be back for you and our son, just wait for me".

For Robert this was the hardest part, leaving his family to work in a foreign land unsure of his fate. As he stepped out at their gate he never looked back because he does not want his wife and their son to see him in his teary eyes. He immediately took a cab right after crossing their street.

"Where are we going sir?" asked Mang Garo a 50 yr old gray haired father like driver. "Please drop me at the Centennial Airport, I have a flight to catch at 9am". Answered Robert. "Umm, would you mind sir if I ask you some questions?" "No, not at all, go ahead", says Robert.

"Sir which place are you going?"

"I'm flying to Dubai because they say that Dubai is the Arabian Dream, a land of opportunity, I want to try my luck", Robert said.

"Oh I see, I'm not wondering if a lot of our people are going abroad due to hardships of life in our country". "I've been with a lot of people, as a cab driver, whom I dropped and fetched at the airport".

While the driver was talking, Robert was imagining the life and the challenges he is about to encounter in the foreign land. He also can't help to think about his wife and their 1-year old son. Every minute spent without them is like a century.

"Oh, I can see by your eyes that this is your first time, am I right sir?" asked the driver.

Robert responded, "yes this is my first time to work abroad".

"I feel sad because I have to be away from my family for two years(minimum contract) I'm nervous too because I don't know the future that awaits me in Dubai. I also feel excited because I know that Dubai is a great place for opportunity, to fulfil my dreams for my family.

Having heard this, the driver empathized with Robert. "I can understand your feelings right now. Throughout my life as a cab driver I've seen a lot of successful people who made it in abroad and achieved their dreams. Although some went home empty-handed. Or even worse, they have become a victim of circumstances in a foreign land. But I can see in you eyes your determination and persistence. I know you'll be successful...

"He looked at the cab driver nodded and hoped it will come true.

> *Jeff believes that true success is winning all areas of life...*

When they arrived at the Centennial Airport Robert went straight to the Overseas Workers' section (Robert was a direct hire, refer to page 31) to get his documents from his agency. Everyday there are thousands of overseas workers being deployed in different parts of the world. On one side it's good to see that Filipinos are considered as world-class workers and can compete internationally. But on the other side of the coin, it's also a hard and harsh reality that our country is loosing a lot of talented and skilled professionals and individuals to other country in which they could have contributed to the progress and development of their mother land.

Now Robert is seated on row 23A economy class of the airplane. On that flight includes variety of people from different walks of life. In the $1^{st}$ class cabin are the high-ranking executives and officials of some of the prestigious companies. You'll find here CEO's, President's of Organizations while in the business section includes some entrepreneurs, highly paid professionals like lawyers, doctors, engineers, architects etc. And Robert is situated in economy (paid by his employer) where you'll find mostly are tourist, frequent travellers, employees, and a lot are just transiting via Dubai to other cities. This goes without saying that in Dubai you'll find a lot of people from different parts of the world with different motivation but have one mission – to become successful.

"This is your Captain Paolo speaking, welcome to flight EK 101. We are now about to depart in few minutes and we expect to land in Dubai at 5am – 4 GMT". We'll be flying in 35,000 feet with a speed of 563mph. We may expect few turbulence so follow all the safety directions from our cabin crew. Just sit back, relax and enjoy...

After few minutes the plane took off the ground. Robert glanced at the window as the plane ascends. He can see that the view outside become smaller as they go up. And now all he sees are vast of clouds covering the horizon… and his dreams waiting in the foreign land.

While on the flight an American guy beside Robert noticed that Robert kept on looking at the plane's window.

His name is Jeff Gibbs. An American guy from California but he is based in Dubai. He got married to a Filipina and that's the reason he is accustomed to some of the Filipino cultures and values.

Jeff is a life-coach by profession and has established his own learning institution in Dubai. Jeff believes that true success is winning all areas of life in which he has achieved already and now he is sharing and teaching it to other people.

"Hi I'm Jeff Gibbs. I can see from your eyes your excitement as you keep on starting at the window since we left the ground". Robert replied, "you're right sir I'm pretty much excited on the journey and challenge I'm about to face. At the same time I feel lonely because I have to leave my wife and our 1year-old son back home in order to fulfil our dreams and goals in life. So leaving them was hard for me but I need to do it for our future. Jeff was moved when he heard this.

"Son I like your attitude. I'm sure that you are going to find the opportunity you're looking for. Remember that success is 90% preparation and 10% action".

"So you don't believe in luck?" Asked Robert.

"Luck is the meeting point between opportunity and preparation". You create your own luck son".

"Thank you sir for telling me that", replied Robert.

"I can understand where you coming from because my wife is from the Philippines and I've been to different islands in your country". Explained Jeff.

"Oh really! That's amazing. You know I'm a Filipino and I have never toured my own country, haha".

"So what can you say about the Philippines?" asked Robert.

"Honestly your country is very beautiful. You have all the natural and human resources. But there's one thing I noticed".

"And what is that?" Robert's face wonders.

"I've met a lot of people who are polite and courteous and that's great. IN fact many are humble. But I have also encountered a lot of poor people in your country. And I think one of the reasons why is because your strength has become your weakness."

"Huh? What you mean by that?".

"Filipinos in general are polite and courteous people and can work well. You can work around the world with other people well, but you are not aggressive enough. Son if you want to be successful in this world, you got to be aggressive about your dreams, your goals and your desires.

"But Mr. Jeff by nature, Filipinos are shy type and we try to please and comfort our guest to the best that we can. Plus when we talk, we talk softly".

"Robert, being aggressive does not mean being rude, shouting or even stepping into someone. Being aggressive means being passionate about your dreams, goals, and your mission in life. You're thinking bold and taking every chance and opportunity and not missing 'em." There's a thin line between being humble and timid.

"Oh I see, now I understand.". How about Dubai? Have you been to Dubai before?"

"Yes. I'm actually based in Dubai and I have my own consultancy there.

"Wow that's great", says Robert. "But what can you say about Dubai?"

"Well one thing for sure that Dubai is a safe haven for a lot of people, let alone the tax free income that you'll get. Dubai is really a land of opportunities, that's why some calls it the Arabian Dream. Not only it's a tourist destination but it has become a global hub for business, trade, media, I.T., aviation and financial services, etc.

"That's wonderful!" says Robert.

"But Robert you have to find out for yourself what Dubai is for you. Because I've been in Dubai for 15 long years and I've seen a lot of stories (both sad and happy) being blinded by their own success. Just to share with you, I have reached success before in a different perspective. I thought success can be measured only by money and by material things. And I took for granted everything I had because I thought that once you're on top of the world you will always remain there. and I was wrong! As fast as I went up to my own definition of success I fell down swiftly. And I don't want you to fall on the same trap Robert. It was a hard lesson for me". But expect a lesson of your own.

(Silence)

Note: Robert fell asleep while jeff is explaining

"Mr. Jeff I think I'm getting a lot of important insights from you within just a short period of chat, but I think I have to relax first and enjoy the view (looking outside the window) though I want to say thank you for sharing with me all your wisdom".

Jeff replied, "Ok you bet as the old saying goes that the best of life is free and that's what I'm giving you for now, a free advice. I'll send the bill later". "Haha", they both laughed.

Then Jeff hands his business card to Robert. "Anytime you need my help I'm just a phone call away". Jeff told Robert. "Thanks sir, I appreciate it", said Robert. Robert puts the card on his wallet and noticed a message at the back: "IF YOU WANT TO HAVE A CHANGE IN YOUR LIFE ACT NOW...YOU ARE IN CHARGE OF YOU LIFE". But this statement didn't ring any thoughts to Robert at least not at the moment.

Now the meals are being served by the beautiful, smart looking and cabin crews. They began serving at the 1st class cabin followed by the business class and the last but not the least, the economy class where majority are located.

This goes without saying that even on board people are categorized according to their status in the society. And the same is true in Dubai. You'll see a lot of ultra rich people in Dubai ranging from Sheiks, Kings and leaders of different countries, up to the top businessman and executives of the world.

Across the city you'll find as well many professionals in various fields such as bankers, engineers, doctors, lawyers, accountants, managers, real estate professionals and many other high-paying jobs. These individuals enjoy huge salaries and fat bonuses plus other benefits like medical insurance, accommodation, yearly ticket allowance, education allowance, profit sharing, etc.

Not all are lucky enough. We also have individuals who earn only minimum and do not enjoy the same benefits as mentioned above, but deserve the same treatment and respect from the society. We may categorize them without any discrimination as blue-collar job ranging from service crew, construction labourers to house servants(maid, cook, driver, etc.) and some even work for royal families.

But in Dubai, which is considered as a 1st world country, having a huge-paying job does not guarantee that you are a money-smart. Often, the people who earn a lot are being lured by the luxuries of Dubai life. As opposed to the individuals who earn only minimum but manage to save and invest.

"This is your captain speaking please remain seated and fasten your seatbelts we are about to land in few minutes". Its 4:45 in the morning (Dubai time – 4GMT).

Robert stared at the window. Finally after nine hours we have reached Dubai.

Wow what a magnificent view, exclaimed by Robert. Robert was viewing the famous Sheik Zayed Road hundreds of meters from above. All he sees are bright lights coming from roads and buildings. It looks like a map of lights which reflects how organized the city is.

As the plane continues to descend, Robert has witnessed how beautiful Dubai is at night time. And he imagines how much more during the day.

Now everyone on board feels the landing of the plane, when the wheels touch the ground. All passengers are smiling and excited to get off, you can pretty much tell by their faces and reactions.

> *But in Dubai, which is considered as a 1st world country, having a huge-paying job does* not guarantee that you are a money-smart

"Hi everyone! This is your captain speaking. We just landed in Dubai and its exactly twenty one hundred hours local time. The temperature outside is a bit warm at 40 degrees. In behalf of my crew and my deck officers, we thank you for flying with Emirates us and enjoy your stay". (Emirates Airlines is the flagship carrier of Dubai)

All passengers began to pack up their belongings on board. Before Robert stood up Jeff shook hand with him. And with a smile Jeff's face he told Robert: "Son, nice meeting you and remember all the things I told you". Robert responded, "Sir the pleasure is mine and thank you for your advice". "All the best, remember you're still the captain of your life and you make your destiny.

The two separated as they went down the plane. Little that they know that soon they will cross each other's path again.

As Robert walks along the immigration area he was surprised by the huge number of people arriving in Dubai – A total of 13.2 million tourists visited Dubai in 2014. He witnessed how thousands or perhaps hundreds of thousands of people mixed of tourists and expat workers arrive in Dubai. It's true that Dubai Airport is one of the busiest airports in the world. Dubai is ranked the third busiest airport in the world in terms of international passengers according to Airports Council International's latest figures. The airport serves more than 145 airlines flying to more than 260 destinations across six continents.(put in box)

Robert was met by his sponsor at the arrival after going through a rigid inspection body search and eye scan. He was able to determine his sponsor by the A4 size card bearing their company name.

He was approached by the guy wearing in kondura (Local dress for man). "Hello sir my name is Robert. I believe you're here to pick me up". The local guy greeted him with a heavy English accent.

"Sala malaikom! My name is Farook I'm your P.R.O. I will drop you to your accommodation". "Ok that's great", Robert replied.

Farook took Robert's original passport and advised him to get a copy from the office. (as per UAE law passport should not be kept by the sponsors). He helped Robert with his luggage, and then they proceeded to the parking and got into the vehicle.

Along the road Robert had notice how tidy and organized Dubai is. "So Mr. Robert, how do you find Dubai?" asked Farook. "Well at first when I saw Dubai above the plane I was impressed by how the city is constructed – I mean its bright city lights is like Im viewing a post card. When I got out of the plane I felt very warm so I had to remove my jacket", Robert explained.

"Hahaha My friend you should get used to Dubai heat especially during summer" Farook grinned.

"But don't worry (sadik) it will get a little colder at the end of the year until the early quarter of the year. (The highest recorded temperature in Dubai is 52.1°C (126°F). Rainfall in Dubai is infrequent and does not last for a long period.)

END OF EDIT

"Alhamdulillah", says Farook. "You can say that we have a good leadership in this country. The government is really serious about the developments and progress of the country. So we as a nation and as a citizen of this country enjoy the benefits and we would also like to share it to the world by hiring people globally just like you to give them an opportunity.

"Ok here we are in you accommodation", says Farook. "As you can see it's a flat with a centralized A/C, automatic washing machine, you also have a cable t.v. so you won't get bored. Everything you need is here. If you have any problems just call my mobile".

"Wow this place is really nice sir. (How I wish I could bring my family here) he whispered to his mind. So when I'm going to start to work?" Robert asked.

"Just relax for a moment my friend. I know you had a long flight. Prepare yourself for tomorrow I'll pick you up at around 8 in the morning and you report to the HQ", Farook explained.

"Alright sir see you tomorrow morning", said Robert. "Massalam sadek, see you tomorrow", Farook replied.

Robert was greeted by his flatmates who are mostly Filipinos. There are other nationalities from Asia, Europe, Africa and South America living in the flat and they stay in different floors.

After an hour of discussion and sharing stories with his flatmates he unpacked his things and went to his bed (it's a double deck). And because he was new he has to stay on top of the bed.

Robert now began to ponder if his decision to leave his family for Dubai is a right one. On his first day in Dubai he missed everything back home and felt "homesick".

As he gently closed his eyes to have some rest, he glanced at the picture of his wife and 1-year old son. And tears began to flow from his eyes. He just closed his eyes and imagined his life being fast-forwarded, achieving his dreams for his family and being with them again.

## Dubai History

**A world of opportunity and an incredible journey, Dubai is the world's premier destination for work and play.**

In just three decades Dubai has grown from a humble fishing village and trading dock to a world renowned tax-free business haven. What was once a sun-scorched village occupied by pearl divers and traders is now a highway to the world.

Strategically located at the centre of three continents, Dubai has a market advantage on trade and commerce.

Dubai began its rise into the global community in the early 1970s.

Under the visionary leadership of His Highness Sheikh Mohammed bin Rashid Al Maktoum, Ruler of Dubai and Vice President of the UAE, a modern free enterprise environment has been created. World-class infrastructure, ultra-modern facilities, a highly developed financial sector and a Westernised business approach, Dubai is now well established as an economic powerhouse alongside London, New York, Hong Kong and Tokyo.

## Dubai Facts & Figures

Is one of the seven emirates of the United Arab Emirates (UAE). It is located south of the Persian Gulf on the Arabian Peninsula and has the largest population with the second largest territory by area of all emirates, after Abu Dhabi.

**Coastline:** **1,318 km**
**Local Currency:** **UAE Dirham**

| | |
|---|---|
| **Life:** | **71.5 years** |
| **Independence:** | **2 December 1971** |
| **Legal System:** | **Federal court system** |
| **GNI per capita:** | **US $25,000** |
| **Main export:** | **Crude oil, natural gas, re-exports, dried fish and dates** |
| **Population:** | **2.1M**<br>**Approximately 85% of the expatriate population (and 71% of the emirate's total population) was Asian (chiefly Indian, Pakistani, Filipino, Bangladeshi and Sri Lankan). About 25% of the population have Iranian origin** |

## HICTORICAL TIMELINE

- 1830: Bani Yas tribe from Lima Oasis led by Maktoum family has taken a small fishing settlement in Dubai
- 1892: Dubai became a popular to foreign investors due to tax exemption, population increased and the pearling sector shoots up
- 1930-1940: Decline of pearl industry due to recession leading to Royal feuds and economic and social pressure
- 1958: After the death of his father Sheikh Rashid hails as Dubai Ruler.
- 1959: Sheikh Rashid receives huge financing from Kuwait's Emir to develop the Creek and accommodate big ships. Dubai is now becoming a major trading hub.
- 1966: Oil is discovered in Dubai enticing traders to live in Dubai increasing economic growth.

- 1968: Crude Oil exportation started and dollars from oil products flow in.
- 1973: The Dirham becomes the official unit of currency in Dubai.
- 1980: Dubai's annual oil income decreases to US$3.
- 1985: Emirates Airline is born to become one of the prestigious airline in the region and making Dubai to become a tourist destination.
- 1986:
- 1990: Shiek Maktoum rule over Dubai after the death of his father, Sheik Rashid in the first gulf war
- 1996-1998: A lot of popular annual event were introduced. To name a few The Dubai shopping festival and the Dubai World Cup.
- 1999: One of the tallest hotels in the world, the Burj Al Arab opens, enhancing Dubai's reputation further as a tourist destination.
- 2000: Dubai Marathon was initiated being the most popular marathon on the region
- 2003: Dubai is recognized by The International Monetary Fund and the World Bank, as a financial hub. Also Dubai International Film Festival was born, the most prestigious and glamorous events on the Dubai events calendar.
- 2006: Sheik Mohammed becomes the Prime Minister and Vice President of the UAE, as well as the ruler of Dubai. He updates the Liberal policies of his Maktoum forefathers and develops Dubai further, raising the city's business profile.
- 2013: the United Arab Emirates won the bid to host the World Expo in Dubai in 2020. This will be the first time that the World Expo is staged in the Middle East, North Africa and South Asia

# Sands of Opportunity

***"Success is 90% preparation and 10% action; Luck is the meeting point between preparation and opportunity".***

***Bo Sanchez,***
***author of 8 secrets of the Truly Rich***

According to Mr. Joe Gibbons, a native of Texas U.S.A. one of the pioneers in the Leisure Industry who had built some of the Worlds Famous Leisure Park in the region and in Asia, modern Dubai is like finding gold back in the old days in California. Some folks found some didn't. He has seen the peak glorious days of Dubai till the recession of late 2008 hits. But what inspired him is the boldness and the innovation of the city and the people behind Dubai. "That's what made Dubai on the top – its brevity in facing challenges and breaking the status quo".

On the same day of Robert's arrival in Dubai a man named Donald also arrived at the airport. Donald came to Dubai as a tourist hoping to land a job where he could use his interest in surfing and in diving. You can say that Donald loves outdoor activities so much.

Robert and Donald have different personalities. Both of them come from different walks of life, and they are committed and dedicated on their dreams and goals in life. Robert is more of a phlegmatic type of a person while Donald is a Choleric. Little they know that very soon they will cross each other's path and be on a mission that seems impossible and they will call it: "ONE MINUTE DUBAI".

Donald arrives at the transit desk for his next flight bound to US and as he goes to the scanner he immediately noticed the asian-looking girl, with a shoulder length silky hair, brown eyes, a very fair complexion, and a very angelic face, standing at the scanning machine.

Donald smiled and looked straight in here eyes and the woman smiled back.

'peep'. The alarm sounded. 'Sir please remove any metallic object in your body', the woman said. 'Ah, ok then Donald removed his wrist watch then passes again the machine.

'peep'. 'Oh sir you have to remove everything please'. 'ah alright'. Then Donald removed his belt. Finally all was cleared.

As he passed by the scanning machine and got his things and hand-carry bag, his eyes were fixed and he was stunned by the beauty of the woman. Then he introduced himself: 'Hello ma'm, my name is Donald and I just want to say hi. It's my first time here in Dubai and I'm happy to see you'.

The woman replied, 'welcome to Dubai sir! I'm glad to see you too. But if you can excuse me coz' there are a lot of people I need to attend'. And Donald replied: 'Oh I'm sorry for that, but I hope to see you again so I can know you more. Ill be back here after a week'. 'well let's see', said the woman.

After a week Donald has arrived again in Dubai but this time he is staying three months before he return to his home country.

Donald was amazed by how huge and clean Dubai Airport is and after walking for about 30 minutes, finally he reached the arrival section and he was met by his uncle who sponsored him.

They went straight to the car park and Donald unloaded his stuffs at the compartment-including his surf board and diving gears. The two kept on talking and Donald shared his flight experience to his uncle plus the woman she met at the airport.

'So how do you find Dubai?' His uncle Ben asked. Donald answered, 'I was pretty amazed how clean and organized Dubai is and the Airport is really huge and world class.'

*Dubai has never stopped progressing and developing. It's like this part of the world is never outdated and they want to always be ahead of everyone and be on top of the world',*

'That's true Donald, in fact Dubai has never stopped progressing and developing. It's like this part of the world is never outdated and they want to always be ahead of everyone and be on top of the world', his uncle Ben explained.

'Just look around Donald', and Donald looks from left to right. All he sees are skycrapers and a very wide road. 'Where are we uncle?', 'Right now we are travelling the famous Sheik Zayed Road. Do you know that 20 years back this road was nothing but a lone dessert? But because of the city's fast development and progress, you can now see a world-class road system plus skycrapers on both side.'

'There was a story that one engineer in charge of developing Sheik Zayed Road has told the Ruler of Dubai that in order to finish the road they need to re-route it because it will hit the sea shore. And the Ruler said: 'If by all means you need to move it then move it to complete the construction.'

'Wow! I can sense the determination and boldness of the Ruler of Dubai' – Donald stated. 'You bet', his uncle said. As they travelled the Business Bay area, Donald was stunned by the towering building – Burj Khalifa.

'Is that the world's tallest building?' – Donald asked. 'Yes it is', his uncle responded. 'What an incredible and magnificent structure! Before I just happen to see it on magazines, news and in the pictures, but now I can see it right before my eyes! It's like a rocket ship from a distance reaching the sky.'

Then Uncle Ben headed to Jumeira Beach Road. Since he lives in Jumeira Area, he decided to take Donald for a quick tour in the famous beach in Jumeira sine it's only a few kilometers from Satwa.

Donald was amazed by the smooth and fine sands along Jumeria beach (there are 7 colours of sand in the U.A.E. refer to One Minute Remider).

Before they reach the open beach he notices the famous Jumeirah Mosque. 'Uncle what structure is that?' His uncle stopped the car in front of the mosque. 'That is the Jumeirah Mosque, one of the tourist spot here in Dubai'. 'Well to me it looks like more of a palace, because of its beautiful and hugeness in structure. And it's very artistic in design.'

Along Jumeirah road Donald noticed a lot of establishments that caters to upper class market. It's also very common that a lot of spots and flashy cars happen to be on the road. Cars he saw before only on TV and magazines – SL 500 Benz, Ferrari Enzo, Porsche 911, Buggati Veyron, Lamborghini Aventador, Masserati GT, Dodge Viper, Ford Mustang, Nissan Skyline, Aston Martin Vantage etc.

Such cars that only rich can afford but seems pretty normal along Dubai streets.

He whispered to himself: 'One day I see myself driving one of these sports cars'. Within a few minutes he is now walking along Jumeirah Open Beach and can feel the fine and smooth sand touching his feet. Its almost 12 midnight and he observed the calmness of the sea and the serenity of the place.

As he looked up in the sky and views the moon (which rarely appears in the Gulf) he wondered and thinks as to what is happening to the other side of the seashore, probably someone is also on the sea shore looking at the sea.

'You know Uncle I never expected that in a such very developed and progressive city like Dubai, there's still such an amazing place like this that's very quiet and peaceful where you can sit down and pause for a while to meditate and visualize'. Donald explained.

'I agree with you Don. In fact when I didn't have any work yet this used to be my favourite hang-out place to think and ponder'. And Donald just closed his eyes while feeling the breeze of the air plus the sound of the seawaves. It's like music to him.

'Ok Don it's getting late and I know you feel tired, time to rest for the moment. You can go here anytime while you're looking for a job.'

And they went back to the car and left the place. It only took them 5 minutes to reach his Uncle's Villa.

---

It's almost 5 o'clock in the morning when Robert wake up and heard a loud voice coming from the near mosque in their accommodation. His roommate Joseph, a Kenyan guy had noticed him getting up his bed. 'Hey Bro! get used to that sound coz' you'll be hearing a lot of those around the city'. 'And what is that?' Robert asked with curiosity.

The one you're hearing right now in Arabic it's their prayer. They do it 5 times a day. Remember that Dubai though has 100 plus nationalities, and is considered an open city, it still follows a strict rules of Islam. So as a foreigner on this land we have to respect their culture and religion.

Thanks for reminding me, now wonder this place is very progressive. Despite of their success in everything they still preserve their culture and tradition, Robert commented.

Robert prepared for his big day, his first day to report at their office. At exactly 8am Farooq, their P.R.O. picked him up at their accommodation.

Al salam alaikom, Farooq greeted Robert. What did you say? It means peace be with you. Farooq explained. Ah alright, says Robert. Then you should reply with: Wa Alaikom alsalam, meaning, and also with you. Again,

Farooq: Al salam Alaikom

Robert: Wa alaikom alsalam

Good! Now you're learning.

As they reached their head office in Downtown Burj Dubai they were greeted by a security guard at the lobby. Good morning sirs! Same to you, Robert responded.

Then as they continue to walk in the lobby towards the elevator Robert saw a long line of people coming from the other side of the building. He noticed that they are from different Nationalities – Kenyans, Filipinos, Egyptians, Indians, Russians, Chinese, and a lot more they are all wearing business attire-both men and women.

What is the fuss all about? He asked. I believe there's an open day being held today by one of the prestigious company here in the building. Farooq explained. Whoah I thought its only in our country that I can see pile of people lining up for a job. Robert answered.

You're lucky my friend because today you don't need to line up and wait for long hours to get an interview because today you will officially sign your contract and start your career. Farooq told Robert.

Few minutes later Robert found himself in the office of their HR Recruitment Manager.

Hi Robert my name is Amro, I'm the Recruitment Manager for American Food Enterprise. We are a group of Companies that franchise some of the major food outlet here in Dubai and across the Region.

Here in Dubai we are spread all over the city, mainly in the malls and other strategic locations and leisure park. As per your contract you will be a team member and will report directly to your store Supervisor. Your basic salary will be AED 1,000 plus commission and overtime. You are also entitled to a housing accommodation provided by the company, 1 meal per duty, health insurance and air fare ticket will be provided once you finish the 2-year contract. Any questions?

My starting offer is quite different from what I have signed back home and it will be difficult for me to support my family since I have a wife and kid to support. Robert commented.

Sadik forget what you have signed back home. It's up to you how you will spend and budget your money. Whether you take it or not you don't have an option but to sign this contract. A thousand dirham is still a thousand dirham but don't worry as long as you do your job right and the management sees you talents and potential, promotion is not hard to get here in our company. Besides that you have the prestige and privilege to be assigned in the world-class mall and one of the biggest malls in the world, Dubai Mall.

Ummm I guess I don't have that option to refuse besides I don't want to pay the penalty. So if you don't have any reservations Robert you may sign on the contract (written in Arabic and English).

As Robert carefully signs on each page of the document he know that he is making his own history. He is preparing his future by his present action. As explained to him earlier by a guy he met at the plane named Jeff Gibbs.

After the contract signing, he shook hand with Amro. Robert you're now officially a part of our family, Mr. Amro told Robert. Sir thank you and I'll do my best. "Inshalla", Amro exclaimed.

Robert got out of the building and walked towards the Dubai Mall along Emaar Blvd which is only a few hundreds of meters away. While walking again he observed the cleanliness and the order of the surrounding. Then he happened to passed by a public payphone.

He took out some coins from his pocket then dials their home phone number. Phone rings, then he dials again. Finally someone picked up the phone.

> Jennifer: Hello, This is Dizon's residence.
>
> Robert: Honey this is me Robert! How are you doing there?
>
> Jennifer: Hi Honey, I'm happy you called us. AJ is now sleeping. You know hon' It's not easy to tell you honestly I'm missing you and AJ is always looking for you.
>
> Robert: I know, I know but we have to be strong. I'm doing this all for you and Aj. And I'll come back like I promise.

Jennifer: So how's your work? Are they treating you fine?

Robert: Don't worry about me. I just signed the official contract like I told you its not that much but I know God will make way for me to find my luck here.

Jennifer: When you will start?

Robert: I just have to undergo physical health exam because they have a very strict policy here especially if you deal with foods. (Robert heard a loud cry from the other side of the line). Is that AJ?

Jennifer: Yeah he just woke up maybe his hungry or wet. Or maybe he sensed that you're talking to me.

Robert: I miss you both so much. (Then the line was cut off).

Robert tried to look for more coins in his pocket but he used his remaining coins to buy a soda from a dispenser.

This time Robert again felt a bit of homesick. At the back of his mind someone is saying to go back home and be with his family. At least they'll be together. He can live comfortably with his family; anyway he had a good job that he can redeem back home.

But he shook his head and remained steadfast. I have to be strong and determined for my goals and dreams. I'm now here in Dubai – the land of opportunity. It's now in my hands, the ball is in my hands.

He continues to walk until he reached the famous – Dubai Mall. As he enters the mall he was mesmerized and astounded by the interior design of the mall, this is a truly world-class and one of a kind, he commented.

The first detail that caught Robert's attention was the massive and luxurious design of Dubai Mall. With more than 1200 stores plus a hotel that is adjacent to it and a host of world class destination, Dubai Mall is revolutionizing the shopping experience.

Wow, it seems a day is not enough for me to tour around. Anyway my assignment will be here so I guess I have to start getting around in here. Truly this place has the best shopping, entertainment, hotels and tourist attractions to offer. And that's only inside the mall, the outside scenery is even more breathe-taking – Water Fountain show, Burj Khalifa, Souk Al Bahar, The Old Town, The Palace, to name a few.

As he was passing by the food court section at the 2$^{nd}$ level he was surprised to see that there is a separate area for those who are dining in and it's covered by dividers.

Out of curiosity he approached one staff. Excuse me sir, can I just ask you a question? – Sure, how may I help you? – I have noticed that you guys have a separate section for those people eating here. Why is that? – Because today is the start of Ramadan. As you know it is not allowed to eat till evening at public places. But for Non-Muslims they can eat discreetly. – Ah, alright thanks for that info.

Few hours later after strolling around he went back to their office – its only few hundred meters away. Robert waited at the pick up point and at exactly 6pm the company service arrived for the staff and employees of American Food Enterprise.

Back at the accommodation, Robert is resting on his double-deck steel bed looking at the picture of his wife and son. Hey brother waz up? A deep voice echoed the room. It's Joseph (Kenyan room mate) I had a very long day brother. -

That's nice to hear can you share it with me bro? –

Well I just had my orientation with our HR and it was quite ok. I was told about my benefits and salary with incentives. Though the basic is not that attractive but as a start I'm fine with that. –

Not a bad start bro. You know as they say that here in Dubai, you have to start from scratch, and everything else is a stepping stone. –

Guess you're right bro, Robert chuckled.

Suddenly a hard knock started beating at their door. Knock! Knock! Knock! Joseph opened the door.

Yes bro who are you looking for? – I've heard there's a new guy in here. Just wanna say hi to him and maybe I can invite him over to our room. It's my birthday and we're having a little party. – C'mon in he's all yours. (And the gentleman entered their room).

Hi! My name is Albert. My room is just opposite yours. We want to welcome you here in our 'cell'. We treat each other here as brothers. In fact, it's my birthday today and I was wondering if you can join us in our mini-celebration. –Glad to meet you Albert (and extends his hand) I'm Robert and I'm the newest guy here.

Thank you for inviting me but I'm not sure if I could come to your party. Happy birthday though Albert. – C'mon brother, you don't have to stay long. Just meet the other guys grab something to eat and drink, then you can leave.

Umm… (Robert was hesitant) – Just few minutes please, Albert pleaded. – Alright bro I'll join you guys. But I can't stay that long coz it's my first day of duty tomorrow. – Thanks man. – I'll just change up then I will go to your room.

After few minutes Robert went to Albert's room where he met the other guys and he was greeted warmly by the group. He was surprised to see that the room was decorated with some balloons and big lettering on the wall. Plus the improvised light effects and some hip and funky music made it a real party hall. Not to mention the booze that they ordered discreetly. (in Dubai it's illegal to buy alcohol unless you obtain a liquor license).

Indeed, this is their life here in Dubai. Nine hours of hard work then straight to their accommodation. If there is a time to celebrate and have fun, birthday parties or if someone is about to go for vacation are the only time they can do it. Pretty much their everyday life is a routine except for those who are on lived-out. (Some companies offer housing allowance) then it's a different story because they have the time and leisure to go around the city.

Robert you're so quiet why don't you speak up? approached Albert. – I'm fine don't worry, I'm just thinking about my wife and kid. What are they doing right now. And if they are also thinking about me…- Robert it's not the time to sentiment we're here to have some fun even for a few moments. Life here in overseas is not that easy as many would say. They don't know the sacrifices and pain we are going through. Don't worry man you'll get used to it, believe me. – how can you handle such loneliness man? Robert was curious.

You know man I've been in abroad for almost 15 years. When I first went abroad, me and my wife were newly married. But I gotta leave soon coz we have a damn big dream in life. – Alright carry on man. Then when my wife had borne our first angel I was out here kickin' my ass, and that hurts coz I wanna be there at that important event.

Then my second was a jr. Same thing happened man. Every three years I'm back home and building my family. Then with our third kid I finally realized that I got to be with them. Got some handful of cash in my pocket for staying almost nine years in the company. Used that as a money seed to a small business investment. It didn't last though coz me and my wife don't have any business background. – and what happened next? Robert was very eager to know.

Well my wife and I faced the fact that the kids are growing along with the expenses. Let alone the education, clothing and food. So again I decided to go abroad. During those time a new haven in the middle east was all over the ads and media attracting tourist and workers alike. And that's why I ended up here in Dubai. – Whoah! That must have been a very tough decision for you to leave again huh, Robert said looking in the eyes of Albert.

Well, you can say that. If only I have another option back home to support my family and give my children a brighter future then I will no longer be here talking to you right now.

The words of Albert strucked right through his heart. He can fully understand where Albert is coming from. He himself is a family man. The only difference is that Robert can still make some adjustment and timeline to his career abroad. One thing he's sure of – He doesn't want to spend the rest of his remaining career being away with his wife and kid. There's gotta be a way to not fall under this predicament, he wonders. But how? As for him he is just about to start his career path working abroad.

It's almost 5 in the morning and Robert can hear the salah(prayer) coming from the near mosque. He knows that it's still early but he also knew that grace is given to those early birds as the saying goes.

Half awake he make some stretching and exercise then read the holy scripture for his daily bread. Then went to the toilet to take a bath but he was stunned by a long line of people as if it's a line for the movie titanic.

After few minutes finally it was his turn to use the shower room. The next thing you can hear was a loud scream – Aahhh! The water almost burn my skin (he whispered). He realized that it makes sense because of the very high temperature outside. Indeed it's almost 50 degrees Celsius during summertime. So he adjusted the shower's temperature 'till it got cold somehow.

It's exactly 7am and all the company buses are ready to bring all the staffs and employees to their designated work assignments. And all of them hopping on the buses as if they were a battalion of army. This is the usual scenario in the staff accommodation and labour camps in Dubai.

Good morning sir! I'm Robert and I'm reporting for duty. Hi Robert, my name is Ashraf. And I'm the Restaurant Manager here. Glad to meet you sir, exclaimed Robert. Just call me Ra-is (boss in Arabic). Ok Robert I want to be clear with you that here in my store, there are three qualities that I require from my staffs: integrity, talent, and energy. But among the three I value most, integrity, because without it the rest will kill you.

After Robert toured the store with Ashraf;

Yes Rais I got that, Robert nodded. For now go to your supervisor, his name is Ahmed, and you will report directly to him. And Robert went to see Ahmed in the kitchen.

So you're the newbie here? Ahmed asks with authoritative voice. Yes sir! My name is Robert. – And where you from? – I'm from the Philippines, the land of the Orient Pearl. – And I must say that my name is Ahmed and I came from the land of Kings and Pharaohs. We, the Egyptians are always strong and great.

Robert feels a little bit irritated by the gestures of his supervisor, but he just remain cool and calm.

Alright Robert for your first day of work I want you to wash all the dishes (there were mountain of dishes) and after that I'll teach you how to clean the machines and equipments. Then don't forget the floor!

Yes Rais copy that. Robert was very submissive. And that started the first day of his duty.

It's true that Dubai is a land of opportunity and many will argue that it's a haven place. But for the many before luck comes to them a lot of hard work and persistence are needed. And like the 'gold rush' in the early days – some people finds it and some people don't.

Going back with Donald, after a week of enjoying as a tourist, he started submitting his CV to the companies he saw in the ads and online that fits his skills and qualification. During his first few days there was no pressure at all. But now with his visit visa nearing to expire in few days, he's bit worried. His uncle is also checking some companies for any vacancy.

So uncle what's the plan? A few day's left and my visa is about to expire. Donald wondered. – well I guess you would have to make an exit in Dubai. What you mean? Donald was curious. Well it's a pretty common scenario here in Dubai that you'll exit Dubai going to the nearest place, say in Kish Oman, while you new visa is still under process by your new sponsor if someone will hire you.

Ah ok, that makes sense. And if no one will hire me then I guess Dubai is not for me and I'll have to go back home. – Don't lose hope son, be positive and you'll bring home the bacon. – Thanks for your support uncle.

Just a day before Donald's visa expires he got a call from an unknown number. Hello good morning! May I speak with Mr. Donald Cruz? – Yes, speaking this is Donald. – Hi Donald, I'm Sheri and I'm calling for SAGA Leisure Park. Are you available today at 1:00pm? We are inviting you for an interview and assessment exam. We are about to open this month and we need customer service assistant. - Sure I'll be there! Donald responded with a big smile on his face.

That afternoon Donald appeared ahead of his schedule and was able to impress the recruitment officer. So after a series of exams, he was among the finalist. Then came an envelope, slowly he began to open it: Mr. Donald Cruz, 'We are happy to announce that you passed all the qualifications for the said position. We would like to invite you to come back tomorrow for the job offer Truly yours, Recruitment officer.'

Upon returning home he shared the good news to his uncle. Uncle I got something to tell you…- Go ahead. I passed the interview and I got a job offer and we'll discuss it tomorrow. – Wow! That's a good news, I told you. This cause for a celebration. – But I don't know the offer yet, Donald gasped.

Well, let's figure it out when the offer is given to you. Just make sure you're on a win-win situation. His uncle explained. Just accept the offer and we'll figure it out. But don't forget you are scheduled to exit tomorrow night for Kish. – So uncle where are we going to celebrate? Asked Donald. – Well, there is a new restaurant in town named – Carinderia ni Tandang Sora. I heard that the food and price is awesome and the place is cozy. They have authentic Filipino dishes that offer world class taste.

You're the boss uncle. So the two had their dinner at the Filipino Restaurant located in Deira Dubai. The restaurant offers a variety of Filipino foods like adobong manok, chopsuey, grilled squid, sinigang, kare-kare, and a lot more Filipino specialties. And the foods here are truly delicious yet economical. Plus the staffs are polite and courteous.

Early next morning Donald dressed up wearing a black suit and tie – his uncle lend it to him. Uncle Ben do I look good with this suit and tie? Coz' I've never worn on except for my J.S. prom. – Oh, yes you look damn good son! Just make sure that you carefully read the offer, then, if you feel good about it, grab the opportunity. The reason I'm telling you this is because there are some companies here that take advantage of folks like you.

What do you mean uncle? – You see Donald these companies knew that guys like you under a visit visa badly needs a job, otherwise, you're visa will expire. You will accept any jobs and offer you anything so they think that even if it's below your qualification.

In short, if you're not happy with the offer and you don't feel right about it, don't accept it. Remember also that it's not about only the money. – Why Uncle Ben? Isn't the money important? Asked Donald. See money affects everything but you also have to be creative. You should keep growing, keep learning, be creative, save (most especially here in Dubai) and enjoy life. If not go back home and be with your family coz that's important too.

Donald pause for a while thinking deep, as if he was absorbing all the words of wisdom given by his uncle Ben. As he travels to Downtown Burj Dubai by bus Donald noticed one thing about Dubai; Though the city is very well diversified in terms of it's multi-cultural environment, there is still harmony, balance and peace all over the place.

Perhaps this is due to the visionary and discipline leadership of Sheik Mohammed Bin Rashid Al Maktoum et al. Donald also observed a lot of projects and buildings being constructed. This shows that Dubai continues to grow and develop amidst the recession that had hit the region.

Mr. Donald Cruz you will be working as a customer service in the newest and biggest theme park in the region. And we are offering you a package of AED 3500 with yearly ticket plus medical insurance, any questions? – Ahem (Donald clearing his throat) Madam I was actually expecting that the offer will be slightly higher. – Sorry dear, it's either you take it or leave it.

This time two thoughts were speaking to his mind: Don't accept the offer if you're not happy with it; Accept the offer you have nothing to loose beside your visa is about to expire.

For Donald this will be quite a challenge. Because during his entire life, he has never worked for everyone. You can say that he is a happy go lucky type of a person. All he knows back home was having fun and partying. At his age in the mid 20's, he still does not have a clear goal in his life. Worried about their son's future, Donald's parents arranged his papers and talked to Uncle Ben so they can send Donald in Dubai and have some career. But Ben would only agree to go to Dubai if its only as a stopover and he wants to visit other parts of the world.

The lady HR coordinator left him in the conference room and after a few minutes went back.

So Donald are you accepting our offer? – Alright then, I'm on it. – Good then we'll prepare the contract and I'll call you for your training. Good luck to your training and welcome to our company Mr. Donald Cruz. – Pleasure is mine, Donald said.

**MINUTE REMINDER:**

**The colour of History**

**Ras Al Khaimah: White** - Made from sandstone, which has plenty of quartz.

**Abu Dhabi: Light Red** - A lighter concentration of iron oxide.

**Dubai: Red** - A stronger concentration of iron oxide.

**Sharjah: Brown** - Contains some organic material, iron and lead sulphide sediments in the limestone.

**Umm al-Qaiwain: Blue** - The greyish-blue colour comes from iron in its reduced condition. When iron stands in water it does not get oxidised and lends a greyish-blue hue.

**Ajman: Cream** - This colour could possibly come from a lesser quantity of quartz present in silica, or it is possible that the sands have a greater sediment of white coral deposits.

**Fujairah: Black** - The colour black possibly stands for the sand that is obtained from corrosion of gabro rock found in the mountain range in the emirate. (Gulf News Published: 08:57 January 26, 2013)

**Dubai is the essence of a 21st century lifestyle - luxurious and family-oriented. Dubai is located midway between the Far East and Europe which is its major advantage.**

Dubai is a booming real estate market.. Dubai real estate boasts amazing projects such as The Palm and The World - the world's largest artificial island complex, developed with villas, golf courses and holiday resorts.

Voted as one of the World's best holiday destinations and recognized as the gateway to the Gulf. Acknowledged as an emerging commercial hub and one of the most desirable places to live on the planet.

- **Dubai - Pearl of the Gulf**

  Voted as one of the World's best holiday destinations and recognized as the gateway to the Gulf. Acknowledged as an emerging commercial hub and one of the most desirable places for living in Dubai.

- **The City**

  Dubai is a growing, cosmopolitan city. Its laws are strictly enforced. The city is tidy secured. It is the commercial and leisure capital of the Middle East.. Quality of life is extremely high.

- **Climate**

  Dubai has a tropical dessert climate. During Summer (October-June) expect a very hot and humid weather 41 °C (106 °F) and overnight lows around 30 °C (86 °F). Many would love the months of December until March and is considered to be the coolest weather of the year 23 °C (73 °F) and overnight lows of 14 °C (57 °F). A few raindrops rain reaching 150 mm (5.91 in) per year

- **Language**

  English is widely spoken among people living and working in Dubai. Alongside Arabic, English is the language of commerce.

- **Money**

  The currency is the United Arab Emirate Dirham (AED or DHS). It has been pegged to the United States Dollar at a rate of 3.67 for many years to ensure currency stability. US Dollars are widely accepted in major establishments.

- **Visas**

  Dubai has very simple visa regulations (which changes regularly) Thirty-three European, North American and Asian nationalities are stamped in on arrival at the airport, at no charge. Other nationalities can arrange visas through online (dubaivisa.net), hotels or UAE embassies and consulates world-wide. You may visit www.dnrd.ae for visa update

- **Entertainment**

  Bars and clubs flock in Dubai streets and hotel. Alcohol is available in most hotels and at the airport. Both sexes can interact. But display of public drunkenness is not to be tolerated.

- **Freedom of worship**

  Freedom of worship is allowed to all religions.

- **Crime**

  Dubai is one of the top five safest cities in the world. Crimes against a person are extremely rare. Theft is almost non-existent. Lost items maybe returned before you ever reach a police station.

- **Population**

  2.106 million (2013)

**About Dubai Economy**

**If you are thinking about Dubai visit, Please consider the following points**

- **Living Costs**

  Dubai compared to Western Europe is more affordable to live, when it comes to basic needs allowing expatriates to save while having a great quality of life. Petrol is low, food inexpensive and loan rates are based in Sharia.

- **Growth**

  Dubai has grown extraordinarily in its Economy. Compared to other city in the region, Dubai has created stable society by accepting the culture of other nations while maintaining off course its own. The first in the region to set up free trade zones, allowing foreign investors to set up their regional operations here. Not only in trade and manufacturing (Jebel Ali Free Zone Authority –JAFZA), this now extends to the free trade zones of Dubai Internet and Media cities (and shortly Medical City), giving the emirate a technological advantage. Meanwhile investment in tourism has grown significantly. With over 50 four and five star hotels in the city, tourism revenue overtook oil revenue as a part of Dubai's gross domestic product (GDP) for the first time in 2003 – 18% of GDP against 17% GDP for oil. Dubai's GDP increases an average 7.5% a year.

- **Taxes**

  At the moment no income or property related taxes of any kind. There are no business taxes other than the banking industry.

- **Policy**

  Each emirate in the UAE is independent in managing its own affairs. In business, the government of Dubai is committed to liberal, free market policies and to the creation of a business environment conducive to commercial activity.

**Salary and Employment Benefits in Dubai**

- Salaries vary widely in Dubai, depending on your qualifications, and your negotiation skills. Dubai has no minimum wage rates or standardized salaries. Salary packages are mostly dependent on how well you negotiate.

Although, the financial concepts involve several other elements, the quality of lifestyle that you would have in Dubai, depends on several factors, the major ones being cost of accommodation, nature of your lifestyle, and your purchasing power.

- Before accepting any job offer, it is good to check with your employer if you are eligible for free accommodation in Dubai. There are several companies in Dubai that offer lodging in personnel houses free-of-charge, depending on the rank of the employees. It is beneficial to join organizations that offer free accommodation, especially if you're new in town, as housing always comes with food and transportation services.
- **Salary Range in Dubai**
- Often, for supervisory positions in certain industries minimum salary range varies between Dh.5000 to Dh.7000. But, this is right for a single expatriate leading an average lifestyle. But for couples or families, seeking to relocate their family to Dubai, a minimum salary of Dh.10,000 to Dh.15,000 would be required. A lower salary range is acceptable in cases where the employer offers housing benefits (in such case even a salary of Dh.5000 would suffice, depending on how much housing allocation would eat up on one's budget).

## Employment Benefits and Pay Package

- Your employer/sponsor must guarantee a return flight back to your homeland when employment has ceased. Your basic salary must be written in the contract and any gratuity pay must be included as well.
- A 21 days annual paid leave (for the first year) and 30 on the succeeding is followed. Some sponsor may charge you your

own Visa fees and the like; and whereas this can be deducted from your final pay (should you violate your contract), It is a norm that sponsors should be responsible for these fees. So be sure it's written in black and white. Nobody else is going to look out for you, from the offer till the signing of the contract. Once you passed the probationary period medical insurance can either be supplied by the government or some companies contracts w3$^{rd}$ party private insurance coverage. To add, there are a few things to be negotiated as well; they are:

- Allowances for food, housing and furniture, transportation (petrol allowance), furnishings, vehicle and cell (mobile) phones. These are things that are NOT required but can and should be discussed.
- Assistance with relocation costs
- Annual return ticket reimbursed
- Medical insurance – check if they supply private policies or will you be covered by the government of Dubai?
- This is where the haggle time comes. It would be invaluable to you to learn this particular facet of negotiation. Gratuity pay is given to employees who have successfully completed employee fulfilment of the contracts under which they were hired. The fact that this gratuity pay is mandatory is yet another positive benefit of fulfilling your contract obligations. However, if you are terminated for good cause under Dubai law, your gratuity is no longer mandatory. As with most things, there is a limit to how much gratuity pay you can receive in Dubai. It cannot be in excess of what would be the equivalent of your salary for 24 months.
- As I have discussed earlier your ability to negotiate your salary plays a very important role not to mention the perks that comes with it

## Employment or Labour Contract in Dubai

- Don't confuse employment contract over Labour contract in Dubai. To put it simply, Employment Contract is the contract or agreement signed between you and your employer or your sponsor during the hiring and recruitment stage. And this will be translated in both English and Arabic. And in case of any discrepancy Arabic translation will rule over the English translation. So you can cross check the Arabic translation from someone whom you trust. As the old saying goes, read carefully before you sign to avoid any regret

- Whereas Labour contract in Dubai is the contract or agreement submitted to the Ministry of Labour in 3 copies. And failing to submit this contract to the Ministry of Labour it will be very difficult to get a working/residence visa.

## Termination of labour contract

- Termination of labour contract can be done by both parties as stipulated in the agreement. You can either terminate the contract before it expires by showing a just cause or vice versa.
- Can your employer sever the contract before its expiration? There are a whole lot of 'yeses' here. Some of the reasons for which your employer could terminate you are: excessive absenteeism with no valid reason, falsification of application information, if you physically assault someone on the job, if your mistake causes the company severe financial loss, you show up under the influence of alcohol, you violate safety protocols, a court conviction of breaking public morals, or giving away any trade secrets. There are extenuating circumstances to some of these as well as procedures that would have to be followed.

- An employment contract is neither legal nor binding in Dubai if it is not translated into both English and Arabic. Though both English and Arabic are spoken in Dubai, if problems occur with translation, the Arabic text is the one that will apply to the situation. Be sure you know what you're signing; have someone you trust translate the Arabic documents for you.

**Probation periods**

- Probation periods in Dubai are required by law. Usually within 3 to 6 mos your employer can either dismissed you which will result to a 'labor ban '(for a specified time unless a new employment contract will come from a govt owned companies or Free Zones Companies). Or end the probationary period after which your full employment contract will apply.

**Limited and Unlimited contracts**

- A limited term contract is a fixed term contract and is linked to the duration of the UAE residency visa (i.e. two or three years, depending on the employer). It will automatically terminate at the end of term unless terminated earlier by either party, or renewed by both parties.
- An unlimited term contract is open-ended and may be terminated for various reasons under the UAE Labour Law. Unlimited term contracts are viewed to be more flexible and user friendly than limited term contracts. Hence, an unlimited term contract is more commonly used in the UAE than a limited term contract. This is suitable for employees who are intended to be permanent and are not undertaking project work.

## Driving License in Dubai

- You would need to be a permanent resident of Dubai to get a driving license. Plus, you would need to undergo a driving course from authorized driving schools and pass all the test (including the RTA test) and get a no objection certificate from your employer (Dubai limits the no. Of citizens who can drive so the NOC is vital in getting a license)
- Get an eye test from your optician or through your driving school. Your application form would have to be mechanically typed in Arabic. Your driving school can help you with this and with the submission of your license to Road and Transport Authority (RTA); you will then get your temporary license that you need to bring with you during your training. Then you have to pass all internal tests (parking, garage, etc) before you can apply for the theory test. Once you've passed these, you can now proceed to road test. In the road test, you will be given a few minutes to demonstrate your skills, once you've passed, kudos! You may then get your driving license.

## Getting an International Driving Permit in Dubai

- International Driving Permit can be by applied through Automobile and Touring Club of UAE. You must be 18 years and above as well as have a valid driving license. You wouldn't have to get a driving course if your driving license came from any of the Gulf Cooperation countries. If you are from a non-GCC country you will need to get a letter from your embassy about the validity of your license as well as the Arabic translation of everything written in your license if not already written in Arabic or English. All information above are correct at the time of writing and for more updated info you may visit https://www.mol.gov.ae/

# Work and the City

*"The harder I work the luckier I get."*-
Gary Player, the master grand slam champion

**Dubai is the only place in the world where you may find different nationalities and culture – about 190 plus of them. Even one marketing ad says: "It is where the East meets West.**

Dubai is indeed a very fast pace and busy city. With big projects such as the Dubai Metro (about 45 miles (75 kilometers) with driverless, remote-controlled trains on mostly elevated tracks),

Maktoum Airport (AT THE HEART OF DUBAI WORLD CENTRAL IS AL MAKTOUM INTERNATIONAL AIRPORT – WHICH WILL BE THE WORLD'S LARGEST PASSENGER AND CARGO HUB AND CAPABLE OF HANDLING ALL NEW GENERATION AIRCRAFT, and the world (an artificial archipelago of various small islands constructed in the rough shape of a world map, located 4.0 kilometres (2.5 mi) off the coast of Dubai) – to name a few. And some on-going projects like Dubai Land, it's evident that Dubai has become a catalyst to the modern and changing world. It's openness and liberal thinking made their neighboring Arab nation to ponder and stretch out their resources for their developments as well.

One amazing fact about Dubai is that you'll find almost 200 different nationalities that are living and working and touring. Even one marketing campaign says:" It is where the East meets West".

Many will argue that Dubai is still young and fresh. For the past twenty years, Dubai has achieved a tremendous success. Though, like other great countries, it's not immune from the adversary effect of the 2008 global recession.

As we all knew that a "bubble" will keep on growing and will burst into a certain period. Surely it did happen in Dubai. But thanks to the rapid action of it's leaders, Dubai has adopted and was able to cope up with the drastic plunge in the global economy. Simply stated, Dubai has learned a hard lesson and has been slowly recovering with a more conservative approach.

We all get spank when we were a kid. But as we mature in age and experience, we should gain wisdom (I hope this is the case). Dubai is still young and still has more potential just like a kid hungry for his dreams and passions.

Going back to the story, Robert and Donald have started their own career path and adventures in Dubai. Unknown to both of them, soon they will become good friends sharing their failures and success.

Robert started as a team member in one of the food and beverage restaurant. While Donald was assigned in a Leisure Theme Park as a customer service.

One morning at the store while Robert is busy doing the opening checklist, Ahmed his supervisor called him. "yalla! Finish that checklist and go down to basement, coz' we have delivery today". - "Yes sir I hear you".

It was his first time to receive a delivery and he was shocked by the volume of it. Twenty boxes of frozen items, twenty boxes of dry items, plus forty packs of produce items. Ali, his co-team member assisted him in receiving of the items.

'Hey man hurry up, carry all the boxes and put it in the cart. We got less than an hour to finish this all'. – Ali do we do this everyday? I mean receiving all of these stuffs. Robert questions. Get used to it Robert, it's all hard work in here. Do you think working in Dubai is easy…Maybe after few months or even few weeks you'll go back to your home country and cry like a baby. Ali was kinda teasing Robert. He was a bit irritated but just ignored his co worker and carried on to his task.

On the other hand, Donald was assigned at the counter station as a cashier. He was handling petty cash and at the same time he was the first contact point for guest passing by and inquiring about the theme park. He seemed excited and contented in his job, at least for the past few months. And the same goes to many individuals who go to Dubai for a career and job opportunity. The first year of employment (and for some even just months!) seems to be exciting, fun and challenging. But time will come when they get bored, laid backed and not happy anymore at their workplace.

Work-home, home-work, then during rest day the whole day will be spent in doing laundry. Cleaning, ironing. And a little time is left for going in and around the city.

This lifestyle had made Donald bored and he needs some actions and challenges in his life. So one day he asked his uncle. "Uncle are there any organizations or clubs activities I can join in? I feel so bored and I needed some activities outside work". "You know son, here in Dubai we have a lot of activities for your interest and hobbies. From water-sports to outdoor activities such as football, basketball even golf and polo games and Desert Safari. We also held yearly activities like Dubai Marathon, Dubai Airshow, Dubai Cup, Dubai Horse Race and a lot more."

Wow! Are you sure Uncle that all of those you just mentioned are happening here in Dubai? Donald asked with amazement. You bet son! Only you need to fix your schedule and we can do all of those one at a time, Uncle Ben assures Donal. His Uncle added: Plus, off course, you need extra money to experience all of those.

As you can imagine Dubai has not only lived to its prominence and high standard of living. Dubai has also offered the best activities that will suit an individual's hobbies and interest. Ranging from indoor/outdoor sports to special events like Vintage Car show. And they're all world-class. Including the first ever indoor snow ski in the Middle East, the Ski Dubai.

Robert continued to focus and concentrate on his job. Though his supervisor, Ahmed, and some of his arab colleagues sometime are pushy on him.

Robert, yalla! After washing the dishes be on the fry station because Kishore is absent today. Ahmed instructed him.

Yes rise I hear you. – Robert responded. Robert went to the frier straight away after washing all the dishes.

Drop one batch of fries hurry! Ali told Robert. Also drop 2 bags of chicken, 2 bags of steak, 4 bags of beef and prepare 6 cans of cheese. And I want it now ok?

This time Robert was bit rattled because of the continuous beeping he can hear from the fry station. But still under his composure, Robert was able to manage it. He is just few days at work but he can feel the pressure from his colleagues plus the "homesickness" he is still experiencing.

Arriving at their accommodation, Robert dropped on his bed very tired. What a long day. – He gasped. Then his roommate Joseph just arrived shortly after him.

How's you day brother? – Joseph asked - tiring but good. Some folks at work tried to 'kick my ass'. I know they're just picking on me since I'm new. – Don't worry about it brother. It's pretty common here in Dubai, since we are working on a multi-cultural environment.

Just don't let them step on you. – Joseph said. I hear ya' brother but sometimes it really gets my nerves up coz even back home everyone was treating me nice.

"Well you're far from home and remember where in Dubai and you can't please everyone." – Joseph comments. "Good thing we Filipinos by nature has long temper attitude, but at times we explode like a volcano".

'Funny you say that coz I remember watching the CNN news many years ago when Mt. Pinatubo in the Philippines, which is a dormant volcano, erupted after hundreds of years. And the aftermath was so huge and devastated'.

Joseph added: Frankly speaking with a multicultural environment we have here in Dubai, culture-clash is inevitable. For as long as respect is there everyone will have a smooth relationship. – I'll take note of that, Robert said.

Dubai is the only place in the world where different nationalities, about 190 plus, come across and interact at workplace, business, marketplace, airport, etc. Dubai has become a collaboration of people, ideas and lifestyle from all over the world.

Donald was doing great at his newly found job. Until one day, there was one unfortunate incident that happened. While at the counter, there was a group of tourist, about three, who happened to passed by at the theme park and inquired at the counter where Donald was stationed.

Upon approaching the counter, one of the tourist immediately recognized Donald. "Hey Donald is that you?" remember me James? Way back in high school days we used to play basketball.

Then with amazement Donald responded: "Yes off course, how can I forget my old buddy? And I still remember all those nasty stuffs we were doing. Hahaha…both laughed and continued to reminisce their good old days. This means that Dubai also has become a meeting place for some of the old friends and colleagues that have never met for a long time.

After the conversation which lasted for about 5 minutes, Donald explained the Park's products and services. Then he told James and his two friends that they can first stroll around the park to have a look.

Donald let them passed through the visitors and staff entrance and not in the normal guest turnstile. However, one colleague named Amro, sneaked on him and told the duty manager that Donald never asked for the permission for his friend to enter their facility.

Donald was caught off-guard and a memo was given to him a day after the incident. And he was asked to change his assignment.

Donald was transferred inside the park to operate some of the rides. Pretty much in Dubai, especially at workplace, you have to be careful of all of your actions because there will be a lot of people from colleagues who would want to "kiss ass" on you for their benefit.

Then one day, while operating one of the rides in the park, one very fortunate incident happened.

Donald was trying to explain to a corporate group the ride and about the restrictions and precaution. – Ladies and Gentlemen good day to all of you…you are about to experience the most adventurous tour of your life. Any questions?

One lady at the back replied: "Is it scary ride?"

The moment Donald has fixed his eyes at the woman, he remembers the asian-looking girl in her mid 20s. Petite, shiny black hair, a very fine skin like a silk, kissable lips and cute tiny eyes. The same woman he met at the airport, when he first arrived in Dubai

With excitement and nervousness Donald said to the woman: Ma'am let me assure you that you will be safe in the ride and it's not scary, it's real fun. Both of their eyes have locked at each other as if they wanted to talk more than about the ride.

After the ride Donald really wanted to ask the girl if she remember him somehow about their first encounter at the airport. But Donald hesitated, with a mixed feeling of emotions, he's afraid he will be rejected.

Anyhow the group has left the scene and Donald was very upset to himself for not having the courage to ask the girl. He was about to prepare the next ride (doing the standard operation) when he saw an ID and on the picture was the woman named Anna Sato at the airport.

Very quickly he took the ID and endorsed area to his colleague. Normally, any lost and found items are being surrendered to the information counter. But he knew that this is the only chance he can again talk to the woman of his dreams, if by luck they have not yet left the park.

Donald searched for them in all corners and even a shadow of them he didn't see. Then at the last moment when he is about to give up…alas! Donald went to the parking near the park and found them.

He ran after them and stopped them. "Excuse me, sorry to interrupt you but I think this ID belongs to you, Ms. Anna Sato". "Oh yes its me, thank you so much". - Anna sighed.

"You left it at the ride earlier. I was about to give it to our lost and found counter but I really wanted to give it to you personally" Robert said. – Wow that is so kind of you…Robert (Anna looking at his nameplate).

Have we met before? Actually you look familiar. – Anna asked. "Honestly, when I arrived here in Dubai at the airport you were the very first person I talked to". I hope you remember that. Donald said.

"Oh yeah, now I remember you were the guy who made our detector kept on buzzing right?" - Funny you say that, yes that was me. Both were laughing.

So Robert I don't want to be rude but my friends are waiting for me. You know what, let me get your contact details so I can keep in touch with you because I owe you by giving back my ID. It's really a big hassle if you did not find it and personally returned it to me. – Anna explained.

"The pleasure is mine Ms. Anna. Let's just say that you were once lost but I found you". Both smiled at each other.

Donald gave his contact details and that same day Anna sent Donald an sms and that started the romance between Donald and Anna. In Dubai a lot of romance and relationship have emerged.

Some are short others are for long time. As if they found their soulmate here on this city called Dubai.

It is important to note that Dubai has a strict policy on opposite sex with regards to relationship. Being a muslim city, intimate affection outside marriage is strictly prohibited. Although a lot of tourists and expats get away with this, it does not follow that they are exempted for following Dubai's policy.

Now, Robert continues to struggle for his goals in Dubai. With a little pay he is challenged how to survive in the city's high standards of living while achieving his goals in life, plus the money that he sends to his family.

Robert noticed that Dubai has many luxuries of life to offer. Money in Dubai is easy to come and easy to go. He has a lot of coworkers that spend money on things that are not a necessity. Like gadgets, electronics, lavish things and the like.

Robert told himself: "I should live a modest life here in Dubai. Although my salary is not that much I should learn how to manage my money well".

Now Robert had an idea since after work he got nothing to do, to do something on the side. But he has to be careful because doing part-time job in Dubai are prohibited by most of the companies and off course by the Ministry of Labour (offenders are fined heavily).

It seems luck is on his way because one time there was a regular customer at their restaurant who was looking for people who want to do a sideline work. The task was to unpack all the office materials/equipments/furniture from one building to another.

And this gave him extra 100dhs per week for extra 4 hours of physical work. This lasted for few months and helped Robert a lot in sending remittances for his family and to save a little.

One busy weekend, while celebrating Dubai Shopping Festival, Robert was taking order from customer and in the queue is Donald. This will be their first encounter (and many more to come).

Hello sir! Welcome to Taco Ring, may I take your order? – Robert politely asked. – Yes Robert (looking at his name tag) what you can recommend for a big party order? Coz today our management will give us a free meal for each staff and we're about a hundred staff. Donald said.

Wow you must have a very large group huh! Ok try our new product Mexican pizza and taco volcano. It comes with beef, chicken and spick chicken. – Robert recommended.

Alright give me half Mexican pizza and the other half the taco volcano. For the toppings its up to you just have a variety of everything. Plus add the fries and drinks of course. – Donald said.

After paying the bill Donald asked Robert, "Hey bro can you assist me with this? I work at the Theme Park inside the mall and I just need some help to carry all of these".

"No problem sir, let me talk to my manager and we'll send someone to help you at ok". – Robert answered with delight.

"Sounds great, thank you for the effort". Donald said.

Robert's manager, Asharaf, told him to go with the customer.

Robert cashed out his counter and helped Donald with the food and drinks. "Ok sir I will be with you until your workplace". – Just call me Donald its fine.

Upon reaching the park Robert was amazed by the beauty and elegance of the park's facilities.

Wow! You have a world class facility in here. – Robert commented. Thanks for saying that. You can always come and visit here and just look for me. – Donald said.

This started the friendship of Robert and Donald. Donald became a regular customer in Robert's restaurant. At the same time Robert has a place to stay if he wants to relax and have leisure time.

A couple of months have passed. Several days were gone. Many weeks have come. And a hundred of hours and thousand of minutes have lapsed. For Robert it seems a decade since he last saw his family and for Donald he has found a new challenge in his life – his career and a love life. In which he does not have any goals – a happy go lucky person.

In Dubai they say that a lot of people you will meet towards success. Not only people but events, situations and predicaments. Indeed, it's your character-building in process. Dubai can either make or break you as a person.

We don't have a control of the future. But the best thing we can do is to have a control of ourselves. And our future is determined by our everyday action, whether good or bad.

For Robert everything seems to be going well with him – the support of his wife is there plus he got promoted quickly at work. He is now the shift supervisor in their restaurant. And his pay is now a little higher than before. His hard work and dedication are now bearing fruit.

But something came up along the way. There was a new staff in his team named Angie. She was in her early 20s, very young, gorgeous and ambitious. Long black hair, round and expressive black eyes. With a curvy body and a beautiful face. No doubt about it, Angie is a real head turner.

On her first day at work, Robert (now a shift supervisor briefed her about her job description.

"So welcome to my team Angie". Robert delightly said. – "Thank you sir, I'm really excited on my first day and a little nervous at the same time". Angie said.

"Don't worry everyone gets their first time. Besides, we work here as one team. So if you need any help or there's something you don't understand, don't hesitate to ask your colleagues or you can approach me directly". Robert explained.

"I can feel your support sir as well as the team". Angie happily said.

Angie reports directly to Robert. She was first assigned at the back of the house preparing foods, vegetables, sauces, etc. And since Angie is a quick learner and very passionate and dedicated person, later on she became a cahier. The following month because of her superb customer service skills, the restaurant manager Mr. Ashraf, promoted her as the store's Guest Relations Officer - of course, with the recommendation of Robert.

One day while Angie was taking her break, she noticed Robert at one corner of their restaurant, quiet and troubled.

"Hi sir, sorry to interrupt you but are you fine?" asked Angie.

Then after few seconds Robert came back to his consciousness. "Hello Angie, sorry I didn't notice you right away". How are you Angie? He replied back.

"Well sir I'm pretty fine". "But sir I'm more concerned about you, you don't look Ok". You looked very troubled sir". Angie told Robert.

"Yeah you're right". Coz last night I had a little argument with my wife and I just couldn't take some of the words she told me". Robert explained.

"Oh sorry to hear that sir. I don't mean to intercede between you and your wife but maybe it just hit your ego sir. It will be fine sir trust me. Besides, the whole team does not wanna see you feeling down". – Angie confidently assured Robert.

"Maybe you're right, maybe its just my ego". Don't worry I'll be back on track. And thank you for being there even for a few moments". Robert said.

The two got back to their respective positions: Angie in front of their store greeting customers and giving a brochure of their menu and Robert at the counter supervising the other team members.

Then a mall liaison gave Robert an invite for the Fireworks Display event to be held at the famous Dubai Water Fountain. At the same time, a special coverage for "Mr. Spider Man" who will attempt to climb the tallest tower in the world using bare hands with glass suction.

Robert approached Angie. "Hey Angie, what's your schedule tomorrow?" Funny you ask that, you're my supervisor you should know. But I'm off-duty tomorrow. Angie replied.

"Good then, we can both view the event for tomorrow at 8pm to be held at the Dubai Water Fountain. I'm in the morning shift. Robert said.

"Is that an invitation? Coz I would say yes. I would love to see the event plus they say that the Dubai Water Fountain Show is a world-class and one of most magnificent view in Dubai". – said Angie.

"Ok then, we have a deal, or should I say a date?" – answered Robert. "Whatever!" – Angie commented.

Its past 6 in the evening when Robert arrived at the location. One thing he obviously noticed was a huge number of expectators waiting for the said event. They all come from different walks of life and different parts of the world.

Robert phoned Angie.

- "Hi Angie, Robert here. Are you coming at the event tonight?"
- "Definitely! I'm on my way. Sorry if I'm little bit late."
- "Nope its ok I just wanted to check if you're really coming."
- "Just hang in there and I'll arrive in a short while."
- "Ok. Angie take care see you here soon. I'm just in front of the Restaurant, Social House".
- "Bye. Sir Robert"
- "Just call me Robert when we're not on duty"
- "You bet sir. I mean Robert (Angie chuckled)."

A few moment later Robert saw a woman approaching him – in a red blouse and a short skirt, wearing high heels and with a curly hair. Robert's jaw almost dropped and he was stunned by the woman's beauty.

As the woman draws closer, Robert's heartbeat began to pump faster. Now he was able to recognize the gorgeous and rolaptious woman no other than Angie herself.

"Hi Robert, did I make you wait?" asked Angie.

"Nope, I'm fine enjoying the fantastic view". (he was referring to Burj) answered Robert.

"Look at you, I didn't know that you're not only beautiful but you are also stunning and gorgeous!" – Robert commented.

"Don't talk to me like that. Other people might hear you and think that you're crazy" – Angie replied.

"Yeah right. Tonight I'm a crazy man, I'm crazy for you". Robert whispered.

"Don't say that sir. I mean Robert. You're wife might hear you saying that and I don't want to be a trouble for both of you. Angie said in a teasing manner.

"Well let's just enjoy and feel the moment". Look at the top of Burj Angie. (Both of them looked up) Do you know that if you stretch the steel bars used to construct Burj Khalifa, it would encircle the earth by one-third?"

"Wow! Really I didn't know that" – said Angie.

"They say that the tallest tower reaches over 800 plus meters, almost a kilometer high. And you know Angie, my dreams and plans in life are as high as the Burj goes. Said Robert.

"There's no problem aiming and dreaming high, for as long as you stay your head on the ground when you reach it finally. For me all I want is to help my family to get out of poverty. I have four siblings and I'm the oldest. My father died when we were still young. Angie told Robert.

"I'm sorry to hear that. So you mean all of you were left to your mother?" asked Robert.

"Actually my mother went with another man taking our youngest sister. Then I went with our Aunt together with my other sibling.

"Then when I reached 16, I stopped my studies to work. And lived with another relative, separating me from my brothers and sisters. I got to see my siblings and my mom once in a while, and I'm always telling them that one day all of us will be together again". Said Angie.

"Wow, you have a great story to tell (wiping his eyes) you know the great thing about trials and hardships in life, is that once you endure and overcome all of it and become success in the end, it's just a great story to tell". Said Robert.

"Exactly!" Angie nodded.

Both Angie and Robert exchanged and shared personal stories and aspirations in life. And this stated the special bonding between them. It seemed that this new friendship paved way to their respective loneliness due to being away from their family back home.

As the event was about to start, a young couple have approached Robert and Angie.

"Excuse me, would you mind if you take a picture of us? Said the guy.

"Sure, why not?"- said Robert.

Then when he closely looked at the guy, its Donald, the one working at the Amusement Park who is a regular customer at their store.

"Donald it's me Robert. Glad to see you".

"Glad to see you too Robert. Robert I want you to meet Anna, she's my friend and she's working in the airport."

"Hi Anna, pleasure to meet you". – said Robert.

"Same here. I'm happy to meet you". – Anna replied.

Then Robert introduced Angie to their group – Guys, I have here Angie with me. She's one of the best in my team.

Both Donald and Anna greeted Angie warmly. And Angie greeted them back.

"You know Angie, Donald is one of our regular customers. And he always invites me to visit their amusement park in the mall, which is a very great place." – said Robert.

"Wow that is so cool! Wish to visit that place too. Angie responded.

Suddenly after the group has finished introducing among themselves, an upbeat music to the tune of Arabic song has been played heard all over the place.

"Guys I think the show is about to start. Let's pause for a while and enjoy the scene". Donald commented.

After few seconds water began to spur all over the artificial lake, dancing gracefully to the sound of music. Every move, every glide and every shoot of the water up above the sky is perfectly synchronized with the music.

Plus the blending light effect coming from the water surface compliments the whole show.

All you can hear are wows and ooohhh from the crowd, mixed of Arabs, Asians, Europeans, Americans, Africans and Local of course.

And in the finale a long shoot of water fired several meters towering the sky. The crowd has applauded to the spectacular water show embraced with ingenuity. – "A truly work of Art" one tourist commented.

"Guys I think the show is not yet over I've heard there would be fireworks display too. So why don't we look for a place nearby where we can fill our stomach while enjoying the night." – said Donald.

> "Well behind us is a cafeteria, let's all have a seat and get some food and refreshments." – Robert suggested.

So the group went to Social House to eat, drink and knew each other better.

They were in the middle of their discussion when suddenly people started pointing at the Burj. Then the spotlight focused on the man climbing the tallest tower in the world.

> "Hey guys, look at that, a man trying to scale the Burj!" Anna gasped.
>
> "You bet. And he's climbing using his barefoot and hands. I wonder how much time it will take him to reach the top". Donald commented.

Later on, a barrage of fireworks display began to fill the sky. People started to awe in amazement on the spectacular show. Different colors filled the sky – orange, pink, blue, green, yellow, red, etc. as well as various shapes can be seen in the sky.

This symbolizes perhaps the colorful lifestyle and how extravagant Dubai is. Let alone the projects that put Dubai in the global map: Burj Khalifa, Burj Al Arab, The World, Palm Jumeirah, Hydropolis Hotel, Metro, Dubai Port, Dubai Land, Dubai Air Show, Dubai Horse Racing and a lot more.

Simply stated, Dubai would want always to be the best in the world. Making it as an ideal and modern city to live.

Dubai's strategic location, has made it a gateway for the collaboration of mixed ideas, to enhance business economy as well as the people's standard of living. As many would say that only in Dubai where the East meets the West.

MINUTE REMINDER:

## Culture Clash

According to Shameena Shahim, Assistant Professor of Cross Cultural Psychology in Dubai: "It is very important to recognize *cultural differences* as differences and not as deficiencies. Just because we do things slightly different here in the UAE, it does not mean it's worse or better. Sometimes the level of clarity is necessary in terms or rules, regulations, norms, what is culturally appropriate and what is inappropriate because of the division between expats and Emirati population. Expats all over the world regardless of knowing the rules and regulations, how aware they are and how aware they are not, how much they actually mix with the host culture, how much they don't. There is always going to be incidences of deviance or criminal behaviour. So it could be that they could be in trouble while even in their own country".

Compared to other Middle Eastern cities, Dubai provides the most cosmopolitan environment which is primarily influenced by the various expatriate communities that have settled here. It is one of the most liberal cities in the Middle East and is open to many cultures

## Greetings & salutation

- When you enter a room or office, you may find that people greet you with "AS-SALAM ALAIKOM" (peace be with you)
- If you are greeted with "AS-SALAM ALAIKOM", it is polite to answer with "WA ALAIKOM AS-SALAM. (and peace be with you)

**Correct forms of address**

- Shaking hands is customary when people meet or are in introduced. However, it is not normally appropriate for males and females to shake hands
- It is appropriate to address others using MR/MRS. with their family name
- Other forms of address are "SHAIKH, HAJJI" (indicating one who has made the pilgrimage to Mecca), and "SAID" or "SAEID" (Sir)

**Language**

- Learning Arabic will greatly help you in building rapport with Arabic speakers
- Learn at least the phrases of courtesy and respect. This will be appreciated
- It is worth nothing that people fro various Middle Eastern countries tend to speak different dialects of Arabic

**Conversation/Talking**

- It is advisable not to talk to Arabic Women if you are a man, unless you already know each other
- Do not point your finger to a person you are talking to
- It is advisable to be aware that crossing legs or sitting showing the undersides of your feet while talking to someone may be considered as offensive
- Various Arabian cultures and traditions should be highly respected at all times.

**Clothing/ Proper Dress**

- Both women and men should always present a modest appearance, when in public

**Eating/Table Manners**

- All restaurants serve foods in the usual western manner
- During the holy month of Ramadan, do not eat or drink in public or in the presence of Muslims within daylight hours
- Muslims do not eat pork or drink alcohol; therefore it is advisable not to offer them these items

**Prayers**

- Prayers are said 5 times a day, at:

  Dawn Fajr

  Midday: Dhohr

  Afternoon: Asr

  Sunset: Maghreb

  Night: Isha

You may find that Muslims are not accessible for business during prayer times

- Do not talk, play music, or make any form of noise while someone is praying and while the holy Qur'an is being read or played on a cassette, television or radio
- Do not walk in front of someone who is praying
- Do not stare at someone who is praying
- Don not step on a prayer rug if someone is preparing to pray

Holidays and Muslims festivities

- All Muslims celebrate the Eid-alFitr, at the end of the holy month of Ramadan, and Eid-al-Addha (pilgrimage to Mecca, better known as "Haj")
- During the holy month of Ramadan, eating, dinking and smoking are all strictly prohibited within daylight hours

**Social behaviour**

- Do not take a picture of any person (in particular, Arab women) without asking his or her permission first
- Do not photograph military installation, ports and airports facilities without official permission
- Do not bring lewd or pornographic pictures, tapes and magazines/reading materials into the country
- Public display of affection are prohibited; refrain from holding hands, hugging or kissing in public

**Traditional Cultural Aspects of the UAE**

- Hospitality a home away from home for many people from different nations.
- Guests are welcomed with a traditional Arabic coffee and Dates
- Traditional Arabic have a Majlis area where guests are entertained
- Traditional Men and Women dress code.

**It is common for Arab Men & Women to dress traditionally**

- Gitra: A square shaped garment worn on the head

- Egal: A circular black cord that holds the Gitra in place
- Shayla: A scarf like garment worn on the head to cover it.
- Dishdasha: A full length robe
- Bisht: A full length cloak worn on the top of the Dishdasha on special occasions
- Abaya: A full length black robe like garment

**Introduction to Islam**

- Islam is the official religion of the UAE
- The term means: submission of the will of Allah
- The Qur'an is the holy book of Islam
- Islam requires Muslims to follow the 5 pillars of faith;
  1. Shahadah
  2. Salat
  3. Sawn
  4. Zakat
  5. Hajj

A Muslim Society

- Conservative Lifestyle
- Women at work
- Male/Female interaction
- Interacting with children
- Prayers Rooms / The Kaaba direction
- Halal & Haram
- Language Barriers
- Alcohol Forbiddden

- Dress code in public
- The holy month o Ramadan
- The Islamic calendar

## Rules in Dubai

### Alcohol or Liquor

Unknown to many who have not gone to Dubai yet. Non-Muslims are allowed to drink in Dubai on licensed premises (hotels and bars). If you are a resident you can apply for a liquor permit to buy alcohol and consume it in your own residence. But take note this does not mean you can go out of your home drunk. If you get caught drunk in public you will be fined and may end up in jail. So drink and drive is a big NO.

### Bouncing a Cheque

Issuing cheques is a very serious matter in this part of the world, particularly in Dubai. So before issuing such, make sure you have enough fund to avoid over draft and paying hefty fine and being held in a jail. A lot of people have learned the lesson the hard way – arrested, jailed and force to leave the country after they settled the amount. So make no joke about it.

### Dancing in Public

Dancing may be considered as a sports now in the international arena. But to give due respect to the local custom in Dubai, dancing in public is not encouraged. Local custom believe that dancing in public maybe an attraction to both sexes and may end up in harassment. So just keep your moves inside your home or in a proper decorum like clubs or gyms but never in public – for your own safety.

## Dress Code

Dress codes is strictly implements even in the malls. Locals dress appropriately when in public. So when going for a shopping, even for a stroll in the park or walking towards work check that your clothes are of decent length. Showing of too much of skin is not appropriate. Even you're inside the mall you will be asked to leave if you wear inappropriately and there are warning signs. If you are on a beach park or water park, off course you should wear swim attire but make sure you cover the private parts and upon leaving the premises make sure you are properly dressed. Just respect the culture that's the key point here. You don't want to get yourself being told by someone else or by the locals that you are offending them.

## Drink Driving

Again this is a big no-no. There is a strict policy when it comes to drink driving and breaking this you'll end up in jail and worse part is that you may be deported. There is a zero tolerance policy when it comes to drink driving.

## Driving Offences

Traffic rules are also implemented strictly as the city is monitored round the clock by CCTVs and make no mistake about it cameras are around the city and it captures a shot if you over speed on the road (smile and pay the fine) So be familiarize with the roads and its speed limits. So avoid tailgating, street race, or using mobile phones while driving, though you may see these in a daily road scenario but don't get yourself in trouble. As the saying goes - Prevention is always better than cure.

**Drugs**

Dubai airport has one the most advanced facility in the world. so bringing in prohibited drugs would put yourself into trouble and don't think about it. Even some prescribe drugs are illegal to enter the UAE. So I would highly recommend to first check with all authorities if you plan to bring prescriptive drugs or over the counter medicines if they are on the list to avoid further trouble. This goes without saying the bags or items being handed to you by friends or relatives always ask them what's in it to avoid landing in jail or even life imprisonment so make no mistake about it. So be always careful and check the stuffs you are importing to Dubai because regrets always happen in the end.

# Having Fun

*"Life is either a daring adventure or nothing at all."*
*- Helen Keller, The Open Door*

Dubai is made for relaxing. It has championship golf courses, tranquil waters for cruising and fishing, luxurious beaches resorts and heavenly spas. But it has something for thrill-seekers, with varieties ranging from desert safari to scuba diving.

**Beach Parks**

**Dubai has several beach parks including the Al Mamzar beach park, Jumeirah beach park, and Creekside park to name a few. While Al Mamzar park has four pristine beaches, two swimming pools, children playground, fresh water showers and picnic areas to offers, the Jumeirah beach park is known for its large lawned areas and beautiful gardens. The Creekside Park offers barbecue sites, amphitheatre with a seating capacity of 1200, an 18-hole mini golf course, 2 restaurants, several kiosks for refreshments, walking and jogging tracks and exit points for abras.**

The city has a lot of fun and amazing experiences to offer to different people on different occasions. Ranging from unique dining experience to weekend session at Jumeirah Park and Public Beach. Or have a traditional Arabic experience through bastakiya and walk through the old district. Including the best bargain that you may find in Souk Markets across the City. Not to mention the crazy offers in the malls through the year, such as DSF, DSS, Gitex, etc.

Having fun in Dubai can be best experienced at its best with the right budget and right contact or agent.

Going back in the story, Donald and Anna started to build up their friendship that will eventually end up in sweet romance. Although they came from different culture and background, they have their own way or resolving it and meeting in between.

For Robert and Angie they easily got well together. At work Robert shows his concern for Angie by providing her all the support that she needs. In return, Angie shows her best performance to the whole team. Thanks to Robert, who helped her a lot to adjust and cope up in Dubai. And everyday right after work the two spend extra time to listen and share their life with each other.

'Angie are you busy after work'? asked Robert. 'Well, let me think about it'… You know sir it's the start of DSF(Dubai Shopping Festival) today and I'm thinking to go around the mall to see some bargain stuffs. Why you ask? Angie wondered.

Well, I'm just thinking if I can invite you for a movie tonight? I have two complimentary tickets. Watching alone would be boring. But if you're busy tonight then… Angie quickly interrupted, I have an idea.

And what is that? Robert asked.

'Why don't you shop with me first then right after we can go and watch a movie'. Angie proposed

'Sound like a good offer I can't resist'. Said Robert

'Then we have a deal' Angie said with a smile.

Right after work Robert and Angie strolled the mall for best deals and bargains. And this goes the same for the rest of the people n Dubai. In fact Dubai is known as the shopping capital in the region.

From fashion accessories to apparels, electronics, personal gadgets, entertainment systems including video games, not to mention life's luxuries such as jewelleries and flashy cars. You name it Dubai has it - everything. Money is not an issue for as long as you have a credit. Every individual in Dubai seems to be a spender during this occasions, which off course has good and bad effects in the economy.

The lavish spending in Dubai had given a boost in some industries like Retail, Tourism, Auto, Leisure, etc. Conversely, it also put a restraint in the Banking and Financial industries in the long run, because people are spending more than what they are earning. And this contributed to the collapse of the market in 2008.

As the two passed by the mall's gold souk, Angie was astounded when she saw a 22 carat white gold necklace with a pearl pendant.

"How much this cost"? asked Angie. Ma'am this only cost 2500 AED with a 30% discount included. You can try it on". The saleslady responded.

So she put it on and she looked in the mirror.

"Wow! It really compliments your beauty. Robert said. 'Really? Thanks but I don't have enough money to buy it, unless I don't send money back home. Angie told Robert.

"Well I'm sure we can go back here anytime when you're ready to buy it. Right ma'am?(looking at the saleslady) asked Robert. "Off course sir as long as it is still here and available". The saleslady responded with a smile.

"It's ok Robert let's go around and maybe we can find one that will suit my budget". Angie pondered.

They were about a hundred meters away from the jewellery store when Robert excused himself for a toilet, but he discreetly went back to it to buy the necklace that Angie wanted, using his credit card.

Though at back of his mind he is contemplating if he's doing the right thing. But most often than not, 'we base our decisions not by logic but by emotion, and later on we justify our actions by using logic. That's human nature.

"What took you so long"? asked Angie. "Sorry I have to answer a phone call. So where shall we go now Angie? Robert asked.

"I just want to sit down and relax after taking a long walk", said Angie.

"Aha, I have an idea. We still have an hour before the movie starts. So why don't we stop by at the Fountain Show to enjoy and relax". Robert suggested

"Yeah why not? Angie countered.

When the two arrived at the Fountain, the show just got started. So they looked for a perfect view, sat down and enjoyed the breath taking scenery. The show played Spanish orchestra music which emotionally touched both Robert and Angie. This place became their perfect past time and bonding moments.

'Angie, can you close your eyes for a few seconds'? Robert requested. 'And why'? Angie wondered. 'Just do it, trust me'. Robert told her. And he slowly pull out a small box from his pocket.

'You may open your eyes now. Robert said. And Angie gently open up her eyes.

Looking at the box Angie asked, "What is it"?

Why don't you open it and see for yourself". Robert countered.

"You're making me nervous" exclaimed Angie. As Angie opened up the box she was surprise to see the necklace she wanted.

"Oh my… Are you sure you bough this for me"? You should not have bothered. Maybe your family has other needs that is more important more than I do. Angie told Robert.

"Please accept it as a sign of our friendship and for always being there for me". Explained Robert.

"Alright I'm willing to accept it but don't spoil me too much coz' I might ask for some more, haha. Angie said with a smile.

And so Angie and Robert have built their 'love nest' within short period of time. Though at work they remained professional as staff and as a manager. Both of them became intimate and their feelings for each other grew stronger. For many this relationship is an illicit one, especially in Dubai, in which authorities are strict on these matters.

For Angie and Robert they are just being happy spending time together. Their bond paved way to their loneliness from being away from home. For some they call this 'homesickness'. And this become the justification for some who had casual relationship in Dubai.

Anna just arrived at her flat when her phone started ringing. Then she pick up the phone.

- Hello, who is this?
- Hi Anna! This is Donald and I'm calling from work. How's everything?
- "Well I had a long day at work, a lot of demanding guests a the airport".
- Oh I see. Don't worry I'm not going to hold you for long. I just want to ask you If I can take you out to a dinner this weekend.

- Sure why not. I'll check on my schedule and I will confirm it to you.
- Really! So that means yes, right?
- I guess so. See you then.
- Ok bye.

Uncle Ben, it's been a while since we last talked about life seriously. I mean last time you were

Advising me about my career here in Dubai, said Donald.

Yes son, I can still remember that. I'm not that old yet. I can see from your eyes that something is bothering you, Uncle Ben replied.

Can I ask you a question? Asked Donald. Sure son fire it away, Uncle Ben responded.

What are the odds for having a successful relationship towards other nationality here in Dubai? Asked Donald. What you mean exactly? Uncle Ben asked him

'I mean since you've been here for a long time, have you seen or heard two persons coming from different parts of the world who met here in Dubai and ended up being together as a couple'? Robert explained.

'Well first of all you have to understand that Dubai is the only place in the world where you may find different nationalities and culture – about 190 plus of them. Even one ad says: "It is where the East meets West. There would be a lot of differences and culture clash. But one thing we can learn from this is being able to appreciate and respect each and other culture.

Second if you're in Dubai then you better start learning other languages and learn how to adjust with other culture because everyday you'll meet people from different parts of the world – your neighbourhood, work environment, in the market, when you go for a shopping or even in coffee or tea shop, when you watch a movie or stroll in the park. Everywhere you go you will have to mingle and interact with different nationalities". Explained Uncle Ben.

"Now to answer your question, yes I've known folks who met here in Dubai and eventually end up as a couple. They were sad and happy ending stories. I guess it happens in other parts of the world as well. It takes courage and sacrifice to be in that situation. But in the end love conquers everything". Said Uncle Ben.

'Thanks Uncle Ben for sharing your thoughts. Now, I can see clearly my case'. Said Donald.

'And why do you ask these things my son? Are you meeting or dating someone lately huh? Uncle Ben asked.

'Actually I have not dated her yet though I asked her already for one. And from the first time I saw her in my life I knew there's something special about her'. Explained Donald.

'So what's your next step'? Uncle Ben curiously asked.

Well let's see, like you said: It takes courage and compromise for us to get along, the fact that we come from different culture and background. I've made my first move by asking her to go out for a date. I pray everything goes well. Said Donald

On that same day in the evening, Donald received an SMS from Anna confirming their dinner on the coming weekend. And for Donald he could not explain the joy and excitement that he feels inside.

Donald decided to call his friend & buddy Robert.

Donald: Hey Robert, where are you now? Can we meet?

Robert: I just arrived in our accommodation. What's the news?

Donald: I'm so excited and I couldn't wait for the weekend to come.

Robert: And what's so special about the weekend huh?

Donald: You know Anna right? She's the one I have introduced with you at the Fountain Show Event, remember?

Robert: Yup. Carry on.

Donald: Well we know each other for quite some time. But this weekend I have finally ask her for a date and she said yes to me!

Robert: I'm happy for you man, good luck man!

Donald: That's why I wanted to see you now. Since you're like a brother to me maybe you can tell me how I can win her heart.

Robert: Alright buddy come pick me up then, and let's see what we can do about it.

After an hour Donald picked up Robert at his accommodation riding his brand new sports car.

'Wow, you got a cool ride man! Since when you got your car'? Asked Robert. "It's been a week with me. I just used the credit of my uncle and I'm going to pay him monthly." Explained Donald.

So what's the plan? Where are we going? We can talk right here if you want. Said Robert.

'I know a place called, Al Sawaleej. It's a local restaurant where locals gather and relax. Also, we can try their traditional tea and 'sisha'. Donald said.

"Ok let's go and try that place". Robert answered

When the two arrived in the restaurant they have observed that the place is full of locals, chilaxing by having their traditional tea and smoking their favourite past time – sisha. They were also surprise to see how local males greet each other – by rubbing their noses against each other.

Donald called the waiter.

"Masah Al Khair, Ahlan wa sahlan! What would you like to order? The waiter asked.

Donald called the waiter.

"Good evening sir welcome to Al Sawaleej. What would you like to order?" the waiter asked.

*For sure there are a lot of good places here in town like in the Old Town Dubai or in Madinat Jumeriah. Since that would be your first date, it should be memorable and very romantic."*

"Actually were finished with our dinner but we just want to relax and unwine and maybe some light meal will do". Said Donald

"You've come to a perfect place. So I suggest you try our tea while watching a sports or movie on our huge screen plasma TV".

"Also can you bring us sisha 'coz my friend and I want to try it while we are discussing some matters." Said Donald.

"What flavour would you like to have? Apple, grape, or orange". Asked the waiter.

"Really it comes with flavour? I didn't know that!" answered Donald.

"So you were telling me that you have asked Anna for a dinner. And where do you plan to take her?" asked Robert.

"Exactly that's why were here you got to give me some good places where we can go. A place something special and very romantic." Said Donald.

"I can help you with that. For sure there are a lot of good places here in town like in the Old Town Dubai or in Madinat Jumeriah. Since that would be your first date it should be memorable and very romantic." Suggested Robert.

"So what's in you mind?" Donald wonders.

"Uhmmm…Aha, why don't you take her to a dinner at dhow cruise!" answered Robert.

"Have you been there?" questioned Donald.

"Nope. But every time I passed by that Dubai creek area that 'dhow cruise' there looks amazing and very relaxing and romantic. Plus you get to see Dubai at night while cruising". Isn't it a wonderful experience together with Anna? Teased Robert. "You bet it is!" answered Donald.

The waiter arrived after few minutes bringing in the tea and the traditional sisha.

"Sir anything else you want to have?" the waiter asked. "Yes, I think we want to have a shawarma", - said Donald.

"Absolutely, our shawarma here is the most delicious you find in town" boasted the waiter.

"Ok then give us two chicken shawarma while my friend and I will savour the tea and sisha" - Donald exclaimed.

"So how about you? I've been talking about what's happening in my life but you never said anything about yourself". Donald commented.

"Well everything is fine with me. Though lately there's a lot of misunderstanding going on between me and my wife, I guess it's common for long distance relationship" Robert explained.

"How about the girl you introduced to us last time?" asked Donald.

"Are you talking about Angie?" said Robert.

"Yes. You know she's young, beautiful, looks smart and intelligent. You're such a damn lucky guy to have her". Donald grinned at Robert.

"Oh, its nothing. We're just friends, we're only trying to give comfort to each other". Answered Robert.

"Yeah right, a shoulder to cry on." Robert said with a smile.

"I know you're matured enough to handle a situation or a relationship, or whatever the case maybe. But just a piece of advice as you're true friend. As early as now you should know your limits and boundaries. I mean if you guys want to have some fun I'm not against it, it's your life after all. But I just don't want to see your family being ruined. I treat you as my brother."

"I really appreciate you concern for me and for my family", Don't worry I will be fine bro". Robert exclaimed.

"Here are you delicious shawarmas still hot and very fresh, enjoy you meal and just call me if you need anything else" – the waiter said happily.

"Shukran my friend"! said Robert and Donald.

And so the two stayed at the Restaurant until 12 midnight enjoying the food, tea and sisha. For many this is just the beginning of Dubai night life. No doubt a lot of people in Dubai are nocturnal and night-goers. You'll find varieties of entertainment clubs and tea house/cafeterias scattered all around the city. Truly in the Middle East Region, Dubai is the city that never sleeps.

Weekend came and Donald can't wait to see and date the woman of his heart – Anna. He prepared early that day and was very excited. Ana on the other hand was so curious where Donald will take her, for her being in Dubai is all about work and career. It's a dream come true for her to be a flight steward, and working in an airport as a ground staff would be her ladder.

But now Anna's life added some colour and music since crossing path with Donald.

"How do I look girl?" asked Anna to Pam, her roommate.

"You look stunning, you're absolutely going to steal every man's heart tonight my darling". Pam said.

"You bet I would, at least for Donald", Anna commented.

"You know girl if I were a man standing right next to you, then definitely I wouldn't miss the chance to know you, be with you, and be the lady of my life". Pam told Anna.

"Are you crazy? Do you know what you're saying? Whoever think of that must have been out of his right mind." Anna said.

"Well at least you're expecting for some kind of proposal, don't you Ann"? Pam said.

"Proposal for what?" Anna wonders.

"Let's cut the chase, we all know that finding Mr. Right buy here in Dubai is almost next to impossible. Everything seems to be superficial. We're all blinded by the way fast-paced environment that we have here. We forget to slow down at times when needed especially when it comes to personal relationship."

"Very well said Pam, I give my two hands up for that. But you know, I'm not thinking of anything like that. I'm just trying to enjoy Donald's company and if anything will progress to the next level… well let's see, I'll let you know, I promise."

"Whatever girl". Just enjoy the night. – Pam

"Beautiful girl all over the world" (ring caller of Anna's phone) I think that's him already. – Anna

"Alright be safe girl and have fun"- Pam.

"Hi Anna, you look absolutely wonderful tonight!" said Donald. "Oh thank you, and you look great too. By the way is that your ride?" Anna asked.

"Yup, just got it the other day. Donald answered.

"Well you have a very cool ride". – Anna told Donald.

"Thank you. I guess the night is still young so let's explore it.

So the two went off the road and they headed towards the famous Dhow Cruise. Dhow Cruise I known for a very romantic dinner while cruising the city along its creek side. It is where Dubai has started their economic ties with neighbouring countries. From a humble beginning, a sail boat, now Dubai has been a major player in global economy.

"Wow this place is really amazing, I never been here before. I saw it many times, just passing by the famous Deira Creek Bridge. But being here in Dhow Cruise in person is really a different experience" - Anna comments.

"Same for me. It's my first time to be here. I thought of bringing you here since this is our first date, and I wanted it to be very special." Donald answered.

"Well, job well done you have impressed me." And I think I won't forget this place, it's really romantic and relaxing" said Anna.

"Hold on to that 'coz the night has just started. The staff told me that tonight there would be someone playing a violin for us while enjoying the dinner. Isn't that too romantic? Said Donald with a smile.

"You bet it is! Answered Anna.

The cruise started and the buffet dinner is ready. A variety of cuisine are made available continental, Asian, European, and of course Arabic. And the soft and relaxing music compliments the whole thing.

Both sailed down Dubai Creek and took-in the breath- taking sights, whilst slipping on a refreshing drink and savouring a delicious meal prepared on board by an international chef which they were greeted personally. It was truly an elegant and unique air conditioned cruise on board.

"Anna can I tell you something?" Donald said.

"Sure go ahead.

"Being here in Dubai never occurred into my mind. To be honest with you I never knew why I'm here in the first place. But one thing I'm certain of. Since I met you, my life was never like this before. I mean before I had no direction, life seems just an ordinary song. Come what may, easy come, easy go, as they say. But now I started having direction in life. A goal or a purpose in a deeper sense. A goal of spending the remaining days of my life with a girl who changed my life. And that is you Anna. So would you allow me to spend the rest of my life with you?"

Anna was speechless for a few minutes when she heard the words from Donald himself. Their eyes just looked up.

Anna sighed and breath heavily. "Ahh...I dunno what to say Donald, being here in Dubai is a dream come true for me. Since I was a kid I've been dreaming to travel around the world by becoming as a flight steward. And Dubai gave me that opportunity".

"Like anyone else living here in Dubai I was so preoccupied with my work. I was so much focused on my career and tend to forget about my personal life. And when you came into my life you let me realize and appreciate life in a more simple yet deeper level."

Their eyes again looked up each other. There was a complete silence for few moments, but you can hear the fast beating of their hearts.

"Honestly Donald I don't know if what I feel for you is right. But what I know is that I'm happy and feel safe every time I'm with you." Anna said.

This statement of Anna gave Donald some kind of a hope and he felt happy and relieved somehow.

"Thank you Anna for letting me know how you feel for me, and I feel the same way too." Donald replied.

Then Donald gently held Anna's soft, smooth and silky hand and put it above his chest…

"Feel it Anna, every beat of my heart shouts your name. And its saying everyday that my heart can't beat without you." Said Donald.

"Well then tell your heart to keep on pumping, 'coz it might not last long". Anna smiled with a grin.

"Hahaha"… both laughed.

"Seriously I'm a little nervous you know. I mean I've never felt nor done this before. I've come from a very ______ family. We still live by our traditions and culture. Mostly the men of our people are the one who go out and provide food and money in the family while women mostly stay at home to take care of the kids and nurture the relationship." Explained Anna.

"But you're here in Dubai". Donald commented.

"Exactly that's the point Donald! I went here 'coz I have a dream of my own. Though I'm here in Dubai, I always remind myself of our values and culture. And with regards to finding for Mr. Right Guy, my parents would always tell me to look out for a man with dedication, hard-working and a loving heart. She didn't even mention money, power nor fame. I guess once you have those three I've mentioned, the rest will follow". Anna explained.

"What you think?" asked Anna.

"Well, I guess you're right. But one thing I'm sure of you are very lucky to have such a lovely family. As for me I doubt if I'm dedicated and hard-working but I'm a very loving person indeed. Would that be enough for you?" asked Donald.

"Umm…let's see where your loving heart will take us." And both smiled and laughed.

...Both sailed down Dubai Creek and took-in the breath- taking sights, whilst slipping on a refreshing drink and savouring a delicious meal prepared on board by an international chef which they were greeted personally. It was truly an elegant and unique air conditioned cruise on board.

The two had a great time at the Dhow Cruise dinner. For Anna it was such a very romantic chapter of her life, unforgettable indeed. And for Donald this moment paved way to pursue his fervent feelings for the woman of his life. Though he knew that this is just the start of their romantic fairy-tale story, and a lot of challenges and situations they need to overcome.

It was already 12 midnight when Donald dropped Anna into her flat.

"It was really an amazing night I have enjoyed your company". Said Anna.

"Same here, thanks for your time and for trusting me". Donald answered. "I hope this won't be the last". He continued.

"Well for as long as I'm free why not. Besides we all need to relax and have fun as well here in Dubai and not just pure work". She said.

"I agree". Donald replied.

"I really wanted to invite you in our room to have a cup of tea or coffee but all of my roommates are in the morning shift and I don't want them to be awaked.

"Its ok Anna no worries, besides we've been together the whole night and you really made my day complete, Donald said.

"Alrite then time to say good-bye for now", she said.

"Good night Anna and sweet dreams", he said.

"Good night too! And drive home safely. She responded.

A day after their first official date, Donald passed by Robert's store to tell him what had happened.

"Hi bro! how are you doing there?" (talking to him at the counter).

"As you can see a bit busy 'coz I'm making our quarterly inventory report. So how's your date with Anna?"

"Wow! It was really a great night for both of us. I can't help it anymore, to hide my feelings for her." He said.

"So you mean you have made a proposal for her?" Robert asked.

"Well, you can say that in a way…but the important thing is that we're having the same feelings for each other. And I don't want to rush her to make a decision", he said.

"For as long as you get her trust and you always make her smile and laugh surely you'll win her heart, Robert said.

And for the next couple of weeks Donald and Anna are going out together with Robert and Angie as a group. They all had fun during their off from work. At one point they even had a group tour in Wild Wadi Resort and Dessert Safari.

In Wild Wadi they had tried the artificial wave and they were all toppled down by the strong current while on a ski board. All of them also experienced going to the dark tunnel and the most thrilling and exciting attraction – the tall water slide.

While inside the water park, Robert has told the group; "Are we really in the Middle East in a desert-wide country? Coz all I can see are Western people and great water structures. We are like in an oasis."

Then Anna responded with a big grin smile – "You bet you are Brother! This is Dubai!"

For their Desert Safari Tour it was really an unforgettable experience. Driving in and around the edges of the Desert Mountain is definitely going to drive you nuts. All you can hear are the screams and they are shouting in excitement as they go up and down the mountain at full speed.

After the sun sets they've witnessed the traditional belly-dancing while having a good cup of tea and a kebab. It was truly a wonderful night they would always remember for the rest of their lives.

And the fun and excitement continued. Anna, since she is working in the Airlines Industry, got a group coupon package in the Ski Dubai – the 1st indoor snow park in the middle east / gulf region.

Again, Dubai has shown the world how unique and innovative they are. Who would ever think that now it's possible to experience snow in a dessert country?

So now every time you feel that temperature in Dubai is extremely hot especially during summer, you have a place to stay chill and cold.

Once a month Robert, Donald, Angie and Anna go to a disco bar (Embassy, Boracay & Buddha Bar are some of the famous bars in town) where people party and listen to a live band after a strenuous and demanding work.

Name it and Dubai has all the leisure and entertainment you can imagine.

Having fun in Dubai does not always mean extravagant, costly, advanced and modern structures. In fact, riding on the traditional boat ride while crossing the Dubai Creek offers a very modest, humble yet extra-ordinary experience.

With only two dirhams in the pocket the group was able to cross the other side of Dubai Creek. And they shopped around the traditional market of the City – including chains of Gold Souks that offer a bargain price.

And during holidays it is very evident that Dubai is full of people, everywhere you go – not only within the Gulf Region but also from different parts of the world like Europe, Asia, and Africa.

In 2015 Dubai attracted 8.2 million hotel guest on the first seven months.

## MINUTE REMINDER

1. Having fun in Dubai can be best experience by having a right budget and calling your travel agent for bookings.

   You may visit www.dttc.ae for more info or you may call Dubai Tourism at 800-7090.

2. Dubai has a lot of crazy bargain offers the whole year round – such as DSF, DSS, Ramadan and Eid Promotion, Gitex, etc. so always ready you budget for this amazing deals.

3. It is important to have fun and relax in Dubai once in a while since it is a very demanding and fast-paced environment. It is one way to release and manage stress.

4. Dubai, the world's ninth global tourist destination, outgrows cities such as New York, Amsterdam, Kuala Lumpur and Shanghai in terms of the total incoming tourist expected this year. The emirate is expected to draw 7.9 million international visitor this year alone, showing a 17.3 % growth rate as compared to 2010. Dubai has a target of attracting 15 million tourists to the emirate by 2015.

## THINGS TO DO IN THE UAE

### Camel racing

A trip to the camel races arranged during the winter months could be a rich experience for visitors to Dubai.

### Creek Tours

A tour of the creek through a traditional wooden-chow or cabin Cruiser could be another imaginative way of seeing Dubai. There are daytime or evening cruises, apart from food and beverages provided on board plus live music as well.

**Desert Safaris/ Feasts**

The Desert Safaris in Dubai are famous among tourists and are organized as part of group tour, and offer taste of true heart of land of Arabia. Visitors can enjoy the tranquillity of the desert in half-day, full-day and overnight safaris. Visitors enjoy the desert trip as much, as they culminate with spectacular sunset views in the evening, and falcon show followed by a traditional Arabian barbecue enjoyed under the stars. The evenings can further be fun-packed with music, belly dancing, smoking of shisha.

**Helicopter Tours**

Those with love for heights can can view the whole city thousands feet above.

Sky Diving

If you love adventure with high adrenalin you shouldn't miss this. You can now check you bucket list and jump out from the plane while captivating the manmade island The Palm Jumeirah and the Dubai Marina.

**Wadi Thrills**

Wild Wadi is a fun-filled Waterpark perfect for family and located next to the world's most luxurious hotel Burj Al Arab and the Jumeirah Beach hotel. You can find here the Jumeirah Sceirah, which is the tallest speed slide outside North America

**Dubai Zoo**

If you love animals then you should visit this place which is the habitat to various species. Placed near to the Jumeirah Beach, the zoo is the oldest of its kind in Middle East. Here you can find Barbary sheep, Siberian and Bengal tigers, Socotra Cormorants, Arabian wolves and gorillas

**Encounter Zone**

The family-friendly Encounter Zone is located in Wafi City Mall and is the right place to explore the Crystal Maze, to ride an indoor roller coaster, to be horrified in a horror chamber, and to indulge in fun activities for kids of all ages.

**Magic Planet**

Located at the Deira City Centre, this fun land includes several rides and attractions make it a must-visit for kids of all ages. Being the Middle East's largest such indoor complex, the Magic Planet offers a collection of arcade games, Clarence Camel's Adventure Zone, a carousel, a bowling alley, miniature golf course.

**Splash Land**

Surrounding 20 hectares of fun water activities, the Dubai Splashland is a favorite among kids of all ages. The huge fun park has several waterslides, bumper boats, log flume, and even an inner tube hire. After the fun-filled activities at the park, one could visit the Carribbean-style main street area, for relaxing at a café, or ice cream parlour, or visit a gift shop.

**Sand-Skiing**

Visitors who are more adventurous and enthusiastic can enjoy sand skiing down the dunes of Dubai desert. Special skiis are used and high dunes in the interior of the desert are chosen as slopes. Sand Skiing can be arranged based on request, or as part of half-day or full-day safari.

## Dubai Ice Rink

The Olympic-size ice rink boasts of world-class amenities, and the visitors can chase their dreams whether it is learning skating, or perfecting their technique, or playing ice hockey. It is also a great place to just socialize with friends who share similar interests and this venue is open any time of the year.

## Dubai Dolphinarium

It is the first fully air-conditioned indoor Dolphinarium in the Middle East, with a seating capacity of 1350. Visitors can also swim with four dolphins if they wish.

## Dubai Aquarium

Being the world's largest aquarium window, the Dubai Aquarium displays huge Sand Tiger Sharks, giant Groupers, graceful Stingrays and shoals of pelagic fish.

## Sega Republic

The largest family indoor theme park in the region with 9 thrilling rides with more than 2oo video games and fabulous redemption prizes.

## Kidzania

An interactive edutainment centre where children can experience over 80 role-playng professions in mimic of a real city.

## Ski Dubai

Ski down a snowy mountain, in a shopping mall, in the desert.

## At The Top

Ascend to At the Top for breathtaking views.

**Dubai Museum**

Learn about the region's origins at the Dubai Museum.

**Wild Wadi Waterpark**

Dubai's first waterpark is making a splash.

**Gold Souk**

Find treasure at the world's largest gold market.

**The Dubai Fountain**

Enjoy the city's most spectacular free show every day.

**Dubai Creek**

Past and present merge along the banks of Dubai Creek.

**Madinat Jumeirah**

Tradition and luxury meet at Madinat Jumeirah.

**Heritage And Diving Village**

Experience old Dubai's living history through crafts and cuisine.

**Jumeirah Mosque**

Don't miss an opportunity to step inside Dubai's most exquisite mosque.

**Beach Parks**

Dubai has several beach parks including the Al Mamzar beach park, Jumeirah beach park, and Creekside park to name a few. This is perfect for family who like to go for a picnic and outdoor lunch. Great also for individuals who like to go for a walk and just enjoy the nature's view.

## Shopping Tours

Specialized shopping tours introduce visitors to souks and major shopping areas in Dubai and even adjacent Sharjah who have limited time to spend in Dubai. Else, visitors can organize their own shopping expeditions.

# Beyond Threshold

*"No man can hope to control his destiny. The best he can hope for is to control himself..." Frank Harvey on Take that Chance!*

It's almost five in the morning.

Alah...Robert is still sleeping, coming from a disco party last night, when he heard the Morning Prayer coming from a mosque nearby. He's been used to it for almost 2 years and at the same time it is his alarm for waking up, though recently, he had a hard-time waking up early in the morning because of the frequent night-outs, clubbing, tours around the city that he together with Donald, Angie and Anna are having.

It seems having fun and pleasure in Dubai is the best way to detoxify from the robust demand of the city and the busy schedule of each individual-from top executives down to the staffs and crews.

There's nothing wrong with that, for as long as you balance everything. Robert slowly became oblivious that he started to blow up the whole deal. First, his priorities in life – the very reason he came to Dubai is to give a brighter future for his family. But now he became self-centered. When friends or relatives ask for help, his response is always – why me? Don't you have any other person to ask help with?

Also, his financial status is suffering because of bad debts and credit cards. All he know to acquire is liabilities instead of an asset. He was better off as a staff when he started – little income with small expense.

More importantly his spiritual side is deteriorating. Before prayer was his best tool and at least he attends Church Service when he was new in Dubai.

But when all his prayers were answered, he started to slip-away. Blessings started to pour his life and he gave all the credits to himself alone, and no one else even to the Big Man above.

From being a service crew to a store supervisor then promoted as the assistant manager and finally as a store manager in less than 2 years. Who could have not given the credit to himself?

Indeed it was a call-back home.

Hello, Robert here. Who's this?

- Robert it's me Jennifer your wife and I'm with your son. It seems you have forgotten us huh! It's been almost three weeks since you last talked to us. What is happening to you?
- Nothing honey – I'm all goo. We're just so busy these past few weeks. You know, I'm handling a bigger responsibility now. And top management is counting on me. Robert explained
- Well, make sure you're telling the truth. Coz' the last time I checked on your FB account you were having a lots of fun and tome it does not look like you're too busy with your work load. Said Jennifer.

- Oh honey maybe what you saw was from our "team-building". We do that to celebrate my team's success every time we hit our target. – Robert explained.
- You better be right Robert. But who's that girl who's always stay beside you? Why is she there? Asked Jennifer
- Maybe you're referring to Angie. She's one of my staff and she's one of my best crew, nothing else. He said.
- Are you sure she's only your staff and nothing else?
- Trust me hon…you have nothing to worry about okay.
- Okay. One thing Robert my sister just called me up and they needed money badly, it's an emergency, her son was rushed to the hospital. Jennifer said.
- Hon, its not that I don't want to help your family but we have our own problems too. Said Robert.
- Yeah right. You know Robert sometimes I think we're better of when you were still here. We live a simple life yet we are able to give and help to others. Jennifer pondered.

Then the line was cut-off.

Robert internalized everything his wife told him. Hmmm… why should I bother helping them? Do they think that money here in Dubai is fast and easy earned money? Besides we got our own problem. I'm pretty sure they can find someone else to help them.

---

Meanwhile, Donald and Anna were having the best time of their lives together. Though both came from different culture and background, love made them united both in heart and soul.

As usual Donald picks up Anna after her duty.

"So how's your day my lady?" he asked.

"Well nothing unusual so far so good. At least I still love my job". She replied.

"Glad to hear that my dear". He said.

"Thank you. Oh by the way, remember I told you about the internal hiring for cabin crew?" she asked

"yup. So what about it?" he said.

"Well I spoke to my supervisor about it, got his approval and I gave my application. Last thing I knew I'm on the short-list. We're like a dozen but they'll choose only one"

"That's going to be a pretty tough competition, but I'm pretty damn sure it's going to be you". Donald said.

"I dunno. Actually there are also a lot of deserving and capable candidate not just me. – she explained.

"Ok, that might be true but look at you. (he started staring at her from head to foot) you're the perfect candidate. Besides you got all it takes to be the next cabin crew. A strong personality with a sweet character'. Explained Donald.

"Alrite don't make my head become bigger…you can't get me mister for your flowery words, haha" she said.

"No, seriously I believe in you.

And Donald held her hands firmly and stared at her eyes closely.

"Whatever makes you happy, I'm just here to support you". – Donald said.

"Thanks Donald for everything – for the support and care you're giving me". Anna muttered.

"Same here Anna. Thank you also for trusting me". He replied.

"Guess what? I'm taking you to the lighter side of Dubai where we can observe the city in a different perspective. Not only that, I also got tickets for the dolphin show. Isn't it exciting huh?" Donald pondered.

"And where exactly is that place?" asked Anna.

"It is called Dubai Creek Park. Also, we can see the creek side of the city while hanging on the cable car." He said.

"That's cool". Anna replied.

After the dolphin show they went straight to ride in the cable car.

"Aren't they lovely creatures? They're so sweet and cute." Anna muttered.

"Yeah. I find them amazing too. But are they cuter than me?" Donald said joking.

"Yup. Indeed they are." She said. And both laughed.

The time is exactly 6 in the evening. It is still bright though the night is catching up with the day and from their position above. They have a clear view of Dubai – only this time I looks calm, quiet and slow paced.

They have reached the other end of the route near the Creek bridge and their cable car is turning back.

"Anna can I tell you something?" Donald asked her.

"What is it Donald? Is there's something wrong?" she wondered.

"Nothing is wrong Anna. In fact maybe this is the right time to tell you…" and he paused.

"Tell me what Donald?" she asked.

"That I…uhm…that I'm starving and maybe you are hungry too. So once we get down from here let's grab something to eat." Donald told here with a smile.

"Ah ok. I thought there is something else you wanna say." Anna sighed.

"Nope. That's it. Maybe next time around we can also invite Robert and Angie to join us here." Donald suggested.

"Yeah, why not we can come back here with them it would be more fun I guess". She agreed.

(Donald was thinking at back of his mind: "You stupid fool, why you did not propose to her how much you love her. What are you waiting for?").

"Hey Donald are you fine? Co'z you look like you've been stunned". Asked Anna.

"Yes. No. I mean I'm perfectly fine". He countered.

"Well I think we should really grab something to eat". She said.

Robert and Donald went to their favorite coffee house located at the Dubai Mall.

"Man, I'm almost there. I was about to tell her my feelings towards her that I love her so much but I just couldn't". Donald said.

"What's holding you back from telling it to her?" asked Robert.

"I don't know exactly. Because I don't know if she feels the same way too". Donald pondered.

"Maybe you're afraid. Afraid of rejection and loosing the one you loved most". Robert told him.

"I think you're right. I'm afraid of loosing her if I tell her my true feelings at least for now I'm happy being with her."

"I hope she feels the same way too. Donald said".

"But bro', till when you're going to hide your true feelings? Asked Robert.

"Well, for as long as it takes". He replied.

"Wake up man! Live your life to the full, life is short. If you really love her then go get her, tell it. Before it's too late". Robert said.

"Is that the reason why you're going out with Angie? You wanted to have the best of both worlds, so you're playing". Donald told him.

"How dare you say that to me? I didn't plan it or choose it, it just happened. She came into my life just as exactly when I needed someone." Robert said with a defensive voice.

"Yes you do Robert. We all make our choices, we make our own decisions in this gift called life". Donald explained with conviction.

"In one way or another you would have to choose in the end. It's just a matter of time my friend". He added.

"In that case I guess I would just like to say that I'm happy just the way it is right now, same as you are", Robert answered.

As time passes by, so the same goes for Robert, Angie, Donald, and Anna. Their love and fairy tale continued.

After few months Anna got promoted as a cabin crew. And thanks for the motivation and moral support of Donald.

While Donald pursued his passion in water leisure, particularly diving. So he enrolled in a diving class and applied as an "intern" in an indoor aquarium while keeping his day job at the theme park. After his Internship Program he was offered a job as a junior aquarist, and, he later on resigned in his current work and accepted the job as a diver.

Unfortunately, for Robert it seems everything is going against the tide; his finances are suffering due to bad debt and credit card spending for the previous months his team is not getting their targets, he is now irritative and he loose his temper easily. Not to mention the relationship with his family is slowly breaking apart.

Until one day, a serious incident made him realize the situation he's into, only until then he came back to his senses.

Robert and Angie were sitting in front of the Dubai Water Fountain and watching the magnificent show, as they used to as often as possible.

"Robert there's something I have noticed in you". She sighed.

"What you mean exactly?" he asked.

"Lately, you seem to changed a lot. I still remember before, you always have the extra time to share with you staff. But now you can't even give them a big smile and warm greetings". She pondered.

"Is that so? You know that I've been given bigger tasks and responsibilities, since becoming a Restaurant Manager". He said defensively.

"You're right. But it does not mean you neglect about your people. You should know that 'coz you've been in their shoes before". She countered.

"Well for me I've earned wherever I am right now, and it's all because of my hard work and dedication. I really don't care about their lives". He argued with a shrug of a shoulder.

"Robert, remember to stay your feet on the ground while on top, because what goes around comes around, 'Life is full of surprises'. Also, there's one important thing that I want to tell you". Angie muttered.

Knowing you is probably one of the greatest things that ever happened in my life, especially here in Dubai. –and she looks straight in his eyes.

"Alrite, you want to add something?" he asked.

…and I'm so thankful for having you, you are such a blessing… but…uhhmm..

"Are we having a problem here"? he asked with a loud voice.

"Nothing Robert. There's no problem at all. In fact since you came into my life I'm happy and satisfied". Angie said.

"Ok. So there's nothing to talk about then?" he asked with irritative voice.

"Yes there is Robert, you got to listen to me please" pleads Angie.

"Ok baby I'm listening". Said Robert.

"Robert, I can't do this anymore. I mean I love you, you know that but I can't ruin a family". Angie said with a sobering voice.

"Honey you're not ruining a family, in fact you're helping me to become strong in absence of my wife and son". Hey it's ok, my wife does not know anything. Besides, we're far anyway from them. We need each other. No, please don't say it's over". He said.

"Robert can't you hear what I just said? I don't want to do this anymore"...she said with tears in her eyes.

"Tell me if there's anything wrong I have done to you". He asked.

"Nothing's wrong with you Robert". She replied.

"Tell me anything then I'll do it for you". He said.

"Your wife, Jenny, for some reason have gotten my email which I don't know from where, and..."

"And what?" he asked.

"And she asked me if there's anything going on between us". She said.

"Ok so did you reply? What you told her?" He said with worries in his eyes.

"I told her nothing. But she insisted and pleaded to leave you for the sake of your son. And she loves you very much". she said.

"Robert it's a woman instinct and I also feel the same way for her. We got to stop this Robert before it's too late". She slowly stressed on the last two words.

"What you mean?" he asked.

"On the email she said something about your son that he's in a serious health condition".

Having said that it felt a blank face on Robert. Then it was followed by a few minutes of silence. Angie finally broke the silence – "C'mon Robert! Don't you see it? It might be a sign to re-arrange your life, and probably re-arrange ourselves. I knew in the first place that, this…this relationship wont work in the long run. It was wrong to begin with". She said firmly.

"Why my wife never told me that?" He wonders.

"Because you went out of your control Robert. I can sense that in you. Success had taken control of you. You lost time with your family because all you care is about yourself on how to fulfill your own success neglecting other people, let alone your own family". She said with conviction.

"That's not true Angie, I'm working here for my family and I care for you". He said.

"Wake up Robert look at yourself – maybe you're on top of the world now acquiring money, authority and material things. But do you still value the people around you? You have been clouded with superficial things here in Dubai".

"Look who's talking? As far as I can remember I taught you everything here in Dubai and now you're telling me what to do, huh?" Robert said.

"Enough of this discussion, it's going nowhere, until you open up you mind. But the least that you can do now is to fix your relationship with your wife". She said.

Robert suddenly grasped her arms; "but I still need you Angie. Please don't leave me". Pleaded Robert.

But Angie let go of his hand… "I'm sorry Robert but I know this is the best for both of us, bye Robert".

…Angie wait, please let's talk – Robert said as she run away with tears in her eyes.

That night Robert was not able to sleep. He kept on calling Angie's phone but it was switched off.

Next morning he called his wife Jenny and found out about their son's health condition – a possible tumor in bone marrow and Joshua needs to go through a series of scans and therapies.

To make matter worse it seems everything is falling apart from Robert – even his career.

They have received a memo from their office they have been bought out by a larger multi-national company.

The first to get affected are the middle management positions, which includes Robert. It's either they take a salary cut or a force resignation and go back home with some gratuity.

But for Robert both options are not applicable because of his son's situation.

Not satisfied with the options he went straight ahead to their Headquarters.

> Robert: Hi I came here to see Kishor, the HR director
>
> Receptionist: Alrite have a seat and relax yourself. You seem to come here from a very distant place. You look tired and exhausted.
>
> Robert: Oh my friend you never know what I'm going through right now.
>
> Receptionist: Sorry to hear that my friend. Don't worry I know you'll get over with it.
>
> Robert: thanks so is Mr. Kishor here? Can I talk to him?
>
> Receptionist: Ok you may go to his office. It's on the far right side at the end of this hallway.

Kishor: Hello Robert. What's up? How may I help you?

Robert: Pretty much you know I'm here it's about the memo you have sent me.

Kishor: So is there anything that you want me to explain?

Robert: The way it was written was technically well understood. But for me the context is somehow vague for me.

Robert: I mean I did everything I could for the past 3 years for your company. And whether you like it or not because of my effort your operation expanded and I have put substantial profit to your accounts.

Kishor: You're missing the whole point Mr Robert. It's not about your performance or what you have done to the company. It's a decision from the higher management. Don't take it too personal, but that's how it works in business whether you accept it or not.

Robert: But sir…for me everything is personal especially now that I have a 4-year old son lying in the hospital with some kind of a disease and I need to pay the bills. Don't you get me sir?

Kishor: I'm sorry Robert, there's nothing much I can do I'm just following orders and I'm only doing my job.

Robert: This is lame. Please help me sir. C'mon don't you have a son?

Kishor: I'm terribly sorry. Take your time Robert just inform me whether you're taking a salary cut or a graceful exit with gratuity.

Robert: (Sobbing) this is totally unacceptable.

On the same day Robert went straight away to one of the Churches in Dubai. For almost 3 years, the last time he talked to God was when he got this opportunity to work in Dubai. Before entering the church he was somehow doubtful if God will be there to listen to him. For he knew that for a long time he did not bother to thank or talk to God for all the blessings he had received.
Then as if a soft voice was whispering in Robert's ear: "Come to me my son…"

Robert slowly began to walk up until in front then kneeled down. "Lord if you're up there listening please help me. I don't know what to do. Everything seems falling apart in my life. My dreams are turning in a dust piece. My marriage, career, my finances, and now my son are dying with some kind of a disease that's killing him. You know God, sometimes you're not fair. I mean you'll give us everything but then only to take it away. Dear God, if you're really a true God please I'm begging to make my son be cured from that killer disease. If you want I have been so self-centred and greedy if you want you can take my life, in exchange of my son's life. I know lately I have been so self centered and greedy about money and the small success I have grasped. But now I know that you can take it all away just like that because everything came from You my Lord."

If you're listening right now, oh God, guide me and enlighten me and give me hope. Tell me what to do. Just give me a sign.

Back to work, Angie gathered all the staffs and crews and asked for a little help regarding Robert's situation.

"Guys, thank you for showing your support and time. We all know that our boss, (Robert) have been acting strange lately. As we all know he is a man with kind heart and he's always there to support us. Although lately we can see a little change about how he treats us, but it doesn't mean it makes him a less good person". Angie said.

"Ok we got you. So why we're here to day?" – asked one of the staff.

"Yeah. What's the agenda? Another staff butts in.

"I'll cut the chase. For those of you who don't know, our boss Robert is going through a very tough trial right now. I know each of us has his/her own problem. But Mr Robert is about to loose his job because of some business mergers and worse his 4-year old son is sick and has been diagnosed with leukaemia, and he needs to undergo a series of treatments which are costly." Explained Angie.

"Oh Ms Angie we're sorry to hear that". Exclaimed the staffs.

"You know all we can do is to offer a prayer for Mr Robert that he'll go through this and off course we'll let him know that we are here to support him".

"Can I count on you guys? "she asked.

"Ms. Angie isn't it that you're going to be transferred to another site location?" they asked.

"Guys that's true as a matter of fact I'll be assigned to other Emirate. But that doesn't mean I can't support and help him. Truth is, I'm leaving with you guys my whole salary for this month so somehow it can help for the treatment of his son". Angie happily said.

"But Ms Angie how are you gonna survive for the rest of the month?" The staffs were amazed by her action.

"I'll be fine. Don't worry, besides I have a little savings that I can live with for a month. Guys don't get me wrong, I'm not telling you to do the same thing. I'm just going beyond what I can do because Mr Robert has also helped me a lot". Angie said.

"I'm also offering 10% of my salary to Mr Robert's son!" one staff shouted at the back.

"Me too I'll donate a portion of my income" said the other. And the rest follows.

That day a miracle has happened and Angie was so happy with the result of her effort.

Even some staffs talked about it throughout the other branches so help and prayers kept pouring on.

All of these were happening without Robert's knowledge. For many this unexpected turnoff events into someone's life – from top of success to a drop blow of tragedy is the worst thing that can happen to them. And as a result they go into a depression, blaming themselves and never came back. But for Robert he accepted this as a wake-up call to his life. At least the first thing he did was to surrender everything to the 'One Authority' above and let faith go its course. And second was to accept his fault and mistakes for his misconception of success and he was willing to change for the better.

For few weeks Robert and Donald have not met, since Robert received the bad news from their HR and health condition of his son.

Robert isolated himself and most of the time he wanted to be alone to focus on his problems.

While at work he was visited by Donald.

"Hey Robert, I'm so worried about you. You were not answering my calls and you neither bother to call me" said Donald.

"Sorry Donald for not answering your calls and for missing our week-end party sessions lately. I'm just going a very tough situation right now" answered Robert.

"Yeah I know. Angie told me everything. And I am deeply saddened by the turn out of the current events especially you son, Joshua"

"Thanks Donald for your concern" he said.

"So how is he doing? And how are you coping up? He asked.

"Well the doctor said he needs to undergo a series of test including and most likely chemotherapy".

"Aside from the fact that our savings has almost dried up I can't handle the pain and sufferings my son is going through at his young age."

"I'm sorry to hear that Robert, any father would have felt the same way." Donald said.

"No Donald, I'm the one who should feel sorry because maybe I'm just paying for the faults and mistakes I've done in my life lately, especially about me and Angie." Robert sighed.

"Oh brother don't say that. We all go certain trials in life. It's only a matter of where and when and how you're going to handle it." Donald explained.

"But this one right now is too much for me Donald. I can't handle it anymore that's why I surrendered it to God." He said.

"I think that's the best thing you can do right now. But I'm also here to support you my friend.

"Thanks Donald." He said.

"Also if you're gonna ask me I would rather choose to go home rather than to stay here because your family needs you and your presence as well." Donald said.

"I know but if I decided to go back home even with my gratuity pay, it would not be enough to cover the medical expenses of my son." Robert hesitantly said.

"You know my dear friend my uncle Ben once told me: that when you are too focused on a problem and you look at it very closely, the whole picture doesn't make any sense." Donald explained.

"What you mean exactly?" he confusedly asked.

"Ok let me show you something. Close you eyes Robert."

(And Robert slowly closed his eyes)

Then Donald held a mobile phone in his hand, and he moved it very close to Robert's face as if it going to hit his face.

"Alright, Robert you may now open your eyes, and tell me what you see." He said.

(Robert gently opened his eyes)

"Donald I…I can't figure it out. It's like a box with some markings. Is it an eraser? or remote? I really can't tell." He sighed.

"Now I'm going to move it away slowly". He said.

As Donald slowly moved away the thing that he was showing from Robert, Robert was able to distinguish it.

"Aha! It's just a mobile phone." Robert explained.

"Now you figured it out. It's the same concept in our lives. When we look into problems, we may see it as very big, very unpredictable, not comprehensible, because we are too focused on it and we are very close. So it will help if we look at it in a different angle so we may see a different perspective." Donald said.

"Thanks for sharing me you thought. I will try to apply it on my life." Robert said.

"I know is not that easy but you have to remain strong and stand still. Besides, there are a lot of people around you who loves you and supports you. Just like Angie."

"Don't mention that name to me. She left me after everything I've done for her. At least the best that she can do is to console me."

"You're wrong Robert. Angie did an extraordinary thing to show how much she loves you. Perhaps she knew that ending your relationship would be the righteous way to do because she wants you to settle your marriage and family even it means to sacrifice her own feelings and interest." He said.

"And why would I believe to that?" Robert asked.

"Just check it with her today, because she told me that by tomorrow her new assignment will start in Abu Dhabi." He said.

"I'm confused…" Robert sighed.

Then one crew interrupted both of them.

"Excuse me sir, but there's a customer out there who's looking for the manager." The crew said.

"And what does he wants? Did he tell you?" Robert asked.

"Surely he's not complaining coz' he looks satisfied."

"Ok please tell him I'll be there in one minute." Robert said.

"Robert I should leave now to get back to work". "Remember all the things I told you brother". He added.

"Sure I will, thanks for everything Donald. Robert said.

As Robert approached the customer, the guy in an elegant gray suit greeted him and introduced himself.

"Are you the manager of this restaurant?" the man asked.

"Yes sir I am, my name is Robert and how may I help you?" Robert asked.

"Well I am Jeffrey Gibbons and I am a regular customer of yours. I can see how great the service and the foods are here in your restaurant and maybe I can help to make it better."

"What you mean sir?" Robert asked.

"Well, aside from being you avid customer I also own a Training and Development company and by profession I'm a life-coach."

"Wait a minute. Don't tell me you're the same Jeffrey Gibbons I met in the plane almost three years ago?" Robert asked with amazement.

"You bet you're right!" he answered.

"So you mean you were just here eating and passing by our restaurant, without even saying hi to me?" Robert told Jeffrey.

"I was hoping that you're the first one to recognize me. Remember the words I said before we went out of the plane?" Jeffrey asked.

"Umm, kinda. It's a long time ago, but yes I still do remember it. That if I need anything here in Dubai, all I have to do is to give you a call.

"You're right again my son, but I did not hear anything from you since then. I suppose, everything is perfectly fine in you life. Look at you now; you are the Restaurant Manager you have gone too far from the moment you arrived here. Without you knowing it, I've been observing you from the time I saw you here".

"Sir you might be right in saying that, but I'm also about to loose everything I've got. I should have listened to you the first time we met, when you reminded me of things about Dubai." Robert emotionally said.

"It's fine son. Don't be too harsh on yourself. Remember that failures and experiences are the best teachers in life". Jeffrey said.

"I agree sir, and for me it's a very hard lesson to learn. It turned my life upside down". Robert said.

"You know my son, once in my life I also had my own afflictions and I was on a crossroad. I don't know where to go and where to start". Jeffrey said.

"And what happened next?" asked Robert.

"You really want to know?" Jeffrey teased him

"Yes sir that it may give me a perspective" he said.

"Ok are you ready?" Jeffrey asked.

"Yup!" he answered with excitement.

"I have decided to take control of my life and act on it. Now if you want to have a change in you life, meet me at the Jumeirah Open Beach at exactly 6 in the morning." Jeffrey said."

"But isn't it too early?" Robert was hesitant.

"Yes it's early and a good start to change your life. Meet me there, no late and from now on, if you want me to be you mentor, then, you have to follow everything I tell you. And you can call me coach." Jeffrey said.

So at the end of the day somehow Robert felt a little relief. Although he knew that back home his son is fighting with a deadly disease and he is still about to loose his job.

But something inside of him is giving him hope. Akin to a rainbow that appears after a heavy rain. He blew up almost everything in his life: finance, career, his relationship with his family and to God, also his health has deteriorated because of stress.

And Robert is ready to redeem everything in his life. With the help of a man named, Jeffrey, God has answered his prayer to give him a sign of hope.

But is Robert ready to take the next challenge? A challenge that will either make or break his life...

## Cost of Living in Dubai

If you are relocating to Dubai for working on a new project, or are on a promotional job offer, and if you are required to actually reside and work in Dubai, it is best to gain some rough estimate about cost of living in Dubai.

Dubai currently holds the 89th position overall based on latest cost of living index, as the most expensive place in the world for expatriate living, out of 300 international locations. Thus, some expatriates are leaving the city due to the high increase of basic commodities like housing and education. The city is now losing its status as a paradise for many expats.

Minimum wage is something that differs from other areas, in that there is no minimum wage. You are expected to wheel and deal for your salary. Should you land an interview, be prepared to answer the question of how much you expect to be paid. Set a bottom limit so that you don't slip under it. Once you've landed that job, the three factors that will determine your quality of living are: expense of living, your purchasing power and your lifestyle. Without having a handle on the cost of living in Dubai, knowing how much of a salary you need would be difficult. The basic three determining factors for the cost of living are: transportation, accommodations and of course, food. Let's take a brief look at each one of these.

## Transportation cost in Dubai

Traffic is usually heavy in Dubai, with massive vehicle volume seen in Dubai's prime locations, particularly the Sheikh Zayed Street, during peak hours. Transportation, no-doubt is an issue to be considered in Dubai, with business centers being far from residential areas.

If you choose to travel by cab or bus, you can probably travel at Dh.12 to Dh.20 or less daily. Gasoline is quite cheap in Dubai, and therefore travelling by one's own car is still a good option in Dubai. If you can manage to save around Dh.15,000 to Dh.50,000 for an ordinary second-hand car or even as much as Dh.40,000 to Dh.300,000 you can go for brand-new cars. Owning a car is an advantage in Dubai, as far as cost of living is concerned, as the fuel budget is quite cheap, and owning a car is the quickest, and most affordable mode of transportation.

While saving for a car purchase, even renting a car at an average monthly cost of Dh.1500 to Dh.3000 is an option. But, if you neither own a car nor have a valid driving license, the next choice apart from Dubai bus (could cost Dh3.00 to Dh.6.00 by bus, metro trip or abra) or taxis (Dh.12 to Dh.100 for short to long trip within Dubai), is car lifts. People who own cars usually transport friends and officemates to and from work.

Dubai ranks 230 out of 300 international locations in terms of cost of transportation for public transport, vehicle costs, vehicle insurance, vehicle fuel and maintenance including hire/purchase/ lease of vehicle/ public transport service maintenance, petrol/diesel, and vehicle purchase. END OF EDIT

**Accommodation cost in Dubai**

This is possibly one of the largest single expenditure to be considered, particularly in Dubai, as real estate is a booming business here. The expenses of residential buildings have gone up considerably in recent years, given the surge in businesses, expatriate influx, and increased demand for accommodation. With Dubai facing high demand for accommodation, villas and flats and residing quarters have become a scarce resource, owing to increased demand. Therefore, leasing is a large consideration here.

Flat sharing is a fad here for practical reasons. But this works out only for singles. Further a flat can get pretty much cramped with such an arrangement. A rental-sharing arrangement is good enough, as it helps in coughing up the required payment of deposits and advance rentals, as it is shared between individuals.

However, expatriates with families, or singles who require privacy, and can afford to pay the rental of a flat/villa/apartment, and those entitled to housing allowance, have a range of options to choose from, including studios, single, double, triple bedroom apartments, and villas, depending on the budget allocated. The housing rental vary largely depending on the chosen location, be it Deira, or Bur Dubai or Jumeirah.

**House Rental Costs**

The housing budget will depend on one's financial capacity and lifestyle choices. The average rentals (approximate values) are in the following ranges:

Monthly rental for Apartments (studios) – Dh.2000 to Dh.5000

Monthly rental for Apartment (single bedroom) – Dh.2500 to Dh.6700

Monthly rental for Apartment (double bedroom) – Dh.3300 to Dh.10,000 or even Dh.12,000

Monthly rental for villa – Dh.6700 to Dh.25,000

**Food Cost in Dubai**

Food is the least of worries in Dubai. Despite the inflation and bad state of affairs of world's economy, food has continued to remain inexpensive in Dubai meeting necessities of people of all income levels. Food is a wonderful experience in Dubai, with Dubai housing people across the globe, you can get to enjoy all kinds of exotic dishes, be it Indian Biryani or Italian pasta.

But it could be costly to dine out in Dubai's premium restaurants. However, the best part is that there are also restaurants that offer food at Dh.35 to Dh.95 per person. The cost of dining in a cheap restaurant without alcohol for a single person will not exceed maximum of Dh.80. In any case, it would be best to enjoy home-cooked food with vegetables on week days and keep eating out for week-end. Dubai also has several cuisines inspired by nations across the world, and so expatriates get to enjoy their favorite meals just as they would in their home countries.

**Education Cost in Dubai**

Re-locating to Dubai with children of school-going age may prove to be a challenge. The cost of private education is quite high in Dubai, and families with income levels less than Dh.10,000 per month may find their salaries insufficient to meet educational needs, while also meeting demands of a cosmopolitan lifestyle.

It will be good to research few private schools in Dubai before relocation. Further, it is best to be aware that a hike in tuition fee could be expected any time. The directories and profiles of several private schools in Dubai are available online. The schools run by American and British nationals usually have high fees, while few schools operated by Asians are comparatively more affordable.

The Grade School tuition fee usually range from Dh.5000 to Dh.90,000 for a full school year, while the high-end counterpart costs around Dh.100,000. The children will have to learn conversation Arab language for them to communicate with other kids and familiarize with culture of Middle East. Therefore, it may be necessary to hire a part-time tutor, but, there is no standard rate for this, as it depends on one-on-one negotiations between parents and tutors.

However, despite this, the cost of education such as pre-school fees, crèche, high-school and college fee and tertiary study fee in Dubai is still comparatively better in comparison to several other cities, ranking 259 out of 300 international locations in the cost of living (education) index.

**Communication Expenses**

Communication will not be a major issue in Dubai. Within the Emirates, the calls are either free or have very low toll charge for outside calls. The cost of various communications including home telephone rental, call charges, service provider fee, internet connection, mobile/cellular phone contract, and calls are equally expensive on average, in comparison to other cities, and is ranked 167 out of 300 international locations in the cost of living index. Monthly telephone calls including mobile or landline could range from Dh.100 to Dh.1000 within UAE, depending on usage.

**Groceries and Utilities Expenses**

The cost of food, non-alcoholic beverages and cleaning material items, including baby consumables, canned foods, baking, baked goods, cleaning products, cheese, dairy, fresh fruits, vegetables, pet food, ready-made meals, snacks, seafood, spices and herbs are expensive in Dubai, in comparison to other cities and ranks 92 out of 300 in cost of living index.

Majority of the goods here are imported from country of manufacture, and costs more than in their home countries, and hence a small amount of Dubai import duty is levied on these goods. Therefore, one may have to shell out 20 to 50 percent more for goods in comparison to buying the same from home country.

As for household costs, water, electricity, household gas, household fuels, residential taxes on house/ flat mortgage, house/flat rental, and local property taxes are more expensive than in other cities, ranking 33 out of 300 in the cost of living index. The average utilities for water and power per month per person are Dh.100 to Dh.500.

## Clothing

Cost of clothing and footwear including business suits, casual clothing, children clothing, hats, evening wear, inner wear and accessories are comparatively expensive and has been raked 11 out of 300 in the cost of living index. Clothing is comparable to the west, except that they may be a little cheaper due to Dubai's tariff and taxation laws.

## Healthcare

The cost of healthcare in Dubai is quite high, and is now in the process of establishing a solid healthcare infrastructure. It is the most important focus for Dubai at present, and is hoped to improve and get cheaper in future. Therefore, the cost of living index rates Dubai's healthcare as 76 out of 300 international locations, with cost of general healthcare, medical and medical insurance, consultation rates, hospital private ward daily rate, non-prescription medicine, private medical insurance, medical aid contributions, all relatively more expensive in comparison to other cities.

## Furniture and Appliances

The cost of household equipments, furniture and household appliance, including iron, freezer, fridge, toaster, kettle, light bulbs, television, vacuum cleaner, and washing machine are all quite expensive on an average in comparison to other cities, ranking 175 out of 300 on the index.

## Recreation

Wine and dine time and leisure and socializing expenses rank highest next to rents, when it comes to cost of living in Dubai. This is because the Dubai city is designed to make you spend. Professionals go out almost every night after work, and all are busy meeting and networking and they end up dining out frequently as well. Also, cost of books, camera film, cinema ticket, DVD, CDs, sports commodities, and theatre tickets are comparatively more expensive here, as is eating out expenses such as business dinner at a good restaurant, and cost of take away drinks, snacks or fast food. Dubai, being the place for youngsters, is no different from New York or Chicago, when it comes to recreational activities.

## Miscellaneous

Miscellaneous costs pertaining to linen, stationary, and general goods and services, including domestic help, linen, dry cleaning, office supplies, postage, newspapers and magazines, are all quite high in Dubai. Also, the cost of personal care products including hair care, cosmetics, sun block, moisturizers, tablets, toothpaste, and shampoo and such products are all equally expensive on an average in comparison to other cities, ranking 128 out of 300 in the cost of living index.

Therefore, if you want to live the Dubai life, while also not sacrificing your financial progress, the best way to do the balancing act is to be well informed about cost of living here, before considering a re-location.

# Winning – Never Give Up

***"Anyone will succeed in whatever field of endeavour in life by acquiring the same virtues and character that boxing world champions do". – Emmanuel D. Pacquiao, 8th division Boxing Champion, Congressman, Entrepreneur, Philanthropist***

. . . As Robert heard the morning prayer coming from the nearby mosque in their accommodation, he immediately got up to take a shower. For he knew that today is his first coaching session with Jeff Gibbons.

But as he passed by their dining hall area, he noticed a crowd of people in front of a huge t.v. screen watching a live pay per view match as early as 5 o'clock in the morning.

The crowd is a mix of different nationalities – Asians, Africans and even some Arabs are also watching.

"Excuse me my friend who's fight are you watching?" Robert asked one African guy.

"Oh didn't you know that today 'PACMAN' will be fighting against the undefeated champion "Floyd" and this is dubbed as the fight of the century. He is a true living legend, though he is considered as underdog he has done what no one has ever done before to become the only boxer who holds the eight division world title". The guy responded.

"Oh really you mean the 'people's champ' Manny Pacquiao from the Philippines?" Robert was smiled.

"Yes brother, that's what I'm talking about!" the African guy said.

"You know one thing that I admire about this guy, is his humbleness and simplicity. And he is a man of action and not of words". The African guy added.

"So you really admire him don't you?" asked Robert.

"Why not? He is the favorite by many boxing enthusiast. Being an underdog, now the pound for pound king, he is truly the man". The African guy explained.

"You know brother a lot of people doesn't know where Manny came from. All they knew are his fame, world title belts, international endorsements and offcourse his big and fat pay check in each and every game. As a matter of fact Manny Pacquiao is considered as a sports celebrity and ranks among the top paid athletes like Tiger Woods, Lewis Hamilton and Kobe Bryant". Robert said.

"And what we don't know about him? "asked the African guy.

"That's a very good question brother. Robert replied. A very few people know his origin. Manny Pacquiao came from a very poor family in the Southern Philippines. He did everything in life just to put food on their table plate. From vegetable vendor to construction worker and selling of a duck's egg. He did all that, then eventually he ended up in a local amateur boxing fight taking home as less as $2 every time he wins. And now he earns millions of dollars per fight, excluding the pay per view commission, promotion and multiple international brands endorsement but what makes him different is that he gives back to the people all his blessings and he stays grounded. "So you can really see the struggle and hardships in life has been through". Robert said.

"Oh man that is so inspiring and uplifting". He African guy said.

"Indeed all his afflictions in life were transformed into a triumph and life's success". Robert answered.

Suddenly it hit Robert, to everything what he has just said. He realized the trials and hardships that he is experiencing at the moment.

For few minutes Robert remained silent. Until finally the famous ring announcer Michael Buffer started to introduce both corners. "Ladies and Gentleman let's get ready to rumble!"...

> "Anyone will succeed in whatever field of endeavour in life by acquiring the same virtues and character that boxing world champions do".

"On the right corner, weighing 145 lbs. holder of 8 world titles and the reigning WBO welterweight champion of the world. From General Santos City, the pride of the Philippines, Manny 'Pacman' Pacquiaoo! (And the whole crowd in the lobby watching T.V. started to cheer and yell.)

Ranking in one of the top richest Filipinos, Manny Pacquiao remains humble. Aside from being a great boxer considered by the Time Magazine as one of the greatest athletes in 2009 making him as one of the most influential people for the year 2009. He was also included by Forbes Magazine in its annual Celebrity 100 list for the year 2009. In 2012, Forbes listed Manny as the 2nd highest paid athlete with a total earnings of $62 million over the past 12 months

He was also the first Filipino athlete to have been honoured to appear on a pledge stamp.

When asked with his formula for success, Manny often says dedication, perseverance, coverage, extreme self-discipline and prayer are his secrets. He once claimed: "Anyone will succeed in whatever field of endeavour in life by acquiring the same virtues and character that boxing world champions do".

Truly, Manny Pacquiao is one of the best athlete in the world not only in his profession but also to his friends as well. He never flashed his money, never wore gold and diamonds to bag to his friends nor he treated people like they are inferior to him. He kept his same old friends and welcomed them to his mansion and always gives credit to the people and to God who gave everything to Him. It seems that Manny always become successful on what he does –producing movies and hosting tv shows, endorsing commercial retail and sports products, owning businesses and he was also elected as the representative of their lone province. Co-owning a professional basketball team (his favorite sports, apart from boxing). And last but not the least he is now preaching the gospel to churches and every individual that he encounters -even his opponent in his boxing profession!

At the peak of his career, once, he got also corrupted by his own success lurking himself with fame, girls, gamble and alcohol but before it's too late he was able to regain focus in what he believes to be his mission as an athlete, husband and a father, and a good citizen and government official. I guess where all susceptible to corruption once we have the power and money commanding over our life.

Manny is a role model for young individuals who seek success in life, respect for others, and a symbol of modesty and professionalism.

Going back to the game after 12 rounds of boxing (or marathon as other say) the judges look to the score cards…

Ring Announcer: And the winner by unanimous decision, the new WBO welterweight champion of the world and still WBA and WBC welterweight champion of the world … Floyd Mayweather!

As the crowd began to boo when the winner was announced Manny have accepted the reality that he have lost to a a very good tactician and safe fighter Floyd. He knew in fact that it's a home court advantage for his opponent and he is the challenger and it seems that what he trained for was not good enough. In the end what matter is your heart and the true heart of a champion because though he lost but he had won the respect of the many.

Life just like in sports is not all about winning. Surely the wins and losses is just like the ups and downs of life. But the important thing is that you don't give up and you stand up every time you fall.

Robert glanced at his watch, He's got only twenty minutes left to make it on time in his 1st day of training session with his coach, Jeff Gibbons.

When he got in the bus and tapped his bus card it read back-low balance. But he knew that if he get off the bus he'll not make it on time and he doesn't want to spoil the 1st day. Even if he gets a cab it would not be practical for him, especially now that he is on a brink of getting axed in his job.

"I would have to make a gamble on this one…Oh boy what are the chances of not getting caught by the authority?" Robert whispered to himself. He kept thinking of not getting checked by the road's authority. For there are times that they do a random check at some points. Dubai has very strict rules whenit comes to traffic and public fines/violations such as over speeding, jaywalking, eating or drinking in a public transport, and being in a female only zone.

As they reached the next stop, a road officer wearing a local dress started checking each passenger if they tapped their cards. Robert felt a bit nervous but he remained calm. And as the officer approached him…

"Excuse me mister, your card pls." – the officer asked.

"Ahh sir I have it with me but when I tapped it, it says low balance" Robert answered.

"Ok let me scan it then" the officer told him. Then the officer using his gadget to check cards scanned Robert's card.

"Oh mister you are short 40 fils, you should have taken a cab or just walk if you like" the officer said.

"Get down the bus and follow me" the officer added.

"Sir I hope you understand. This is actually my first time to have a low balance. I always recharge my card with enough credit. I know I have a low balance but I will recharge on the next stop when I see one". Explained Robert.

"There is no free ride here mister and now your action resulted into a 200 dhs fine". Said firmly by the officer.

"But sir I don't have that money and I'm also about to loose my job. Maybe you can give me a warning. Pleaded Robert.

"I'm sorry but a rule is a rule especially here in Dubai ticket then surrender me yours I.D. if you have the money you can claim it afterwards". The officer said.

The officer took his details and put it into the system and handed over his ticket.

"Alright mister you can hop in the next bus then just show your ticket to the driver. I hope you learn your lesson". The officer said.

The next bus came after 15mins. And now he is gonna be late surely for their training session.

Robert sent an sms to his coach: "Coach something came up. I had a little trouble on the way I will be late for couple of minutes".

This particular incident just show how really tough the authorities are in Dubai. From pedestrian, traffic and road rules, up to the implementation of simple rule such as no food and beverage in public transportation are strictly enforced. Otherwise, you know the next scenario.

Bear in mind that CCTV's are scattered in and around the City.

Discipline plus law and order have been one of the key factors why Dubai became so progressive on a little span of time.

In fact if you go back in the 90's Dubai is a vast plain dessert with a few buildings along Sheikh Zayed Road.

From fishing and pearl community Dubai has truly emerged and transformed as a hub for various business industries and a role model for developing countries.

Although many consider Dubai as still new and young, it has already put itself in the global map.

And whether you're in Dubai as an expat, tourist or for business, you should take advantage of the opportunity it has to offer.

Their first training session was in Jumeira Open Beach Park. It's almost 6:30 in the morning when Robert arrived.

From the shore you can vividly see the sunrise and it's just perfect for the people getting fit by the beach. The whole scenery creates harmony and serenity against the robust and fast-paced city.

Indeed Robert felt relaxed and peaceful upon reaching the place amidst his current situation. And it all came back to him-his goals and dreams why in the first place he went to Dubai.

Near the water he saw Jeff, and Jeff waved his hand telling him to come near-by.

"Good morning Robert! So how's your day?" asked Jeff.

"Coach I'm sorry for being late. I didn't mean being caught along the way. If I only knew what's gonna happen, I could have put more credit in my card". Explained Robert.

"Beat it Robert! You can't cry over spilled milk. First lesson: Be responsible for your actions all the time and you'll earn a respect. Never put the blame on anyone else even to yourself. Admit your mistake and carry on. We're all humans after all, but make sure you don't fall on the same trap next time around". Jeff said.

"Fair enough Coach." Robert replied.

"Now young man, can you tell me why we are here again. And we're not wasting our time are we? Jeff asked.

"Uhmm, we are here because...I want to have a change in my life perhaps...I mean, it seems everything is out of my control. Everything is falling apart." Said Robert.

"First of all I can sense you're not so sure of what you really want in your life. You seem confused my son. Remember, your present life determines your future. It's called 'FUPRESS'. So whatever decision or actions you do today, it will have a big impact on your future life." Jeff explained.

"So what should I do now with my life falling piece by piece?" questioned Robert.

"Remember son, a big answer is only as good with a big question." Jeff said.

"Huh! What you mean exactly?" Asked Robert.

"Unless you have a big 'why' then everything won't matter. Let me ask you this way: Why would you like to have a change in your life?" asked Jeff.

"Coach isn't it too obvious? My marriage is on the brink of falling apart, and I'm about to loose my job in the coming month or two and the worst part of it, my 4 year-old son is lying in bed with bed with some kind of a disease and I don't know if I can still see him breathing." Robert emotionally cited everything.

"Now we're talking. As I've said you need to have a big 'why' otherwise it won't matter. Now you understand? Asked Jeff.

"Yes coach. And I knew this had happen because of the wrong decisions I've made lately in my life. But all I wanted it to become successful in life. That's why I went here in the first place." Said Robert.

"Ok. Now enough of that whining and blaming part. What I want you to do is take change of you life while there is still time left. Be the scriptwriter of your own life and not just a mere spectator nor an actor." Jeff told him with conviction.

"And how exactly am I going to do that?" asked Robert.

"That's what I'm here for my son. To guide and coach you. I'll show you the right path to success, but at the end of the day it's still you who'll take control and make decisions. Explained Jeff.

"Alright whatever I takes I'll do it coach. Besides I got nothing too loose for this right coach?" Asked Robert.

"Yes there is Robert". Responded Jeff.

"And what's that coach?" he asked him.

"Remember son, a habit or belief is a thousand time more powerful than your decisions in life. No matter how eager you are to make a change or decision in life if you don't act on it, it will just remain an idea. So your habits will play a crucial role on this training."

"Whatever habits or beliefs you have about success we will slowly change it. In short, we are going back to basics like teaching a kid how to tie his shoes or brushing his teeth." Jeff told Robert.

"Wow it seems so easy if it's like that." Robert commented.

"So if you're up to the challenge meet me up again in this place same time. Don't be late or else I'll fine you 200dhs". Jeff jokingly said.

"I'll not let you down coach. But what am I supposed to do for the rest of the day? It's my off today and I thought we're going to have a whole day session." Asked Robert.

"That is enough for today. I'm sure you've learned a lot today. What I want you to do is to go worship and praise spend time with your family and friends." Jeff instructed him.

"But my family is back home coach." Replied Robert.

"Then you can call them or chat with them, what is technology for? If not keeping communications with our loved ones." Jeff replied.

"Thank you coach for your time and see you again till we meet again next time." Robert said.

Robert did exactly what Jeff told him to do. First he went to attend the church service then he went to a computer shop to chat and talk with his family.

Robert: "Honey how are things going out there?"

Jenny: "Oh Robert things are going tough here…Last week we went to see a specialist for Joshua's case and he said that we need to perform the operation because his condition is deteriorating."

Robert: "I know it's hard but we have to hold on".

Jenny: "And until when Robert?"

Robert: "Until God answers our prayers. I don't know how will I explain it by I'm going through a transformation as things are unfolding in our lives."

Jenny: "What you mean?"

Robert: "Right now I know a guy whom I met three years ago in my flight going here is mentoring me. I know honey that I've made a lot of wrong decisions lately in my life. But I thank God because He made me realize that everything comes from Him and anytime He can take it away if you don't take care of your blessings".

Jenny: "Well whatever it is you're going through I support you Robert. I'm just praying that our son gets well soon".

Robert: "Thank you Jenn for giving me another chance. I hope that you can forgive me for my actions. Don't worry I won't fail you again. I have surrendered everything to Him and I know He has great plans for us."

As they finished their talk, Robert felt a bit of calmness in his heart. Though their son is still sick and he is about to be sent home by his employer, he didn't loose hope, thanks for the mentoring sessions with Jeff Gibbons.

Back at work Robert brought back his drive and energy plus his compassion for his staffs.

Then one day his friend Donald dropped by at their shop to tell him a very important message.

"Hey bro can you meet me later at the Café lower ground, I have a very important thing to tell you". Donald said.

"About what? Why don't you tell me now?" Robert replied.

"I'm late at work so I got to go now. It's about Angie, she handed me an envelope yesterday and she wanted me to give it to you." Donald explained.

"Are you sure it's for me? For as far as I can remember the last talk I had with Angie was not a good one, we had an argument and she left me all alone when I needed her". Robert said with a bit of grudge.

"I know how you feel but just check it, you'll loose nothing anyway". He said.

After duty Robert and Donald hanged out at their favourite coffee shop near the Ice Rink. And Donald gave the envelope to Robert. As he opens it and read the letter, tears started falling from his eyes.

The letter goes...

> Dear Robert,
>
> I am deeply sorry for what happened to us. I know that I have disappointed you and you may hate me for what I did – leaving you in the middle of everything. Maybe up to now you're still mad at me and I can't blame you for that. But what I did was the best for all of us. If there's one greatest thing that ever happened to me and that is you – being part of my life. And you taught me that no man

has ever done before. Being with you makes my life complete. But despite the love and care that you have shown and given to me, I cannot fathom the fact that I will be destroying a good family. I don't know how to face your son if he asks me why I stole you from them. So best way to show my love for you is to leave you so that you can still fix what needs to be fixed and correct what needs to be corrected.

And since I know the situation of your son, I have enclosed a cheque which somehow will help to support the operation of your son. It's the little money I have shared plus the help of some staffs across our company.

I tried to raise a fund for your son. And this is the best thing that I can do to show my love for you. Take care and may God bless you.

Yours truly,
Angie

"Bro are you alright? What's in the envelope? Asked Donald.

"I was such a fool, because of my poor decisions on life I have affected people that love and care for me. But I believe this is God at work. Somehow, I see hope and forgiveness". Robert said.

"Whatever it is I hope and pray it has enlightened you". Donald answered.

The cheque in the envelope amounted to almost ten thousand dirham enough for few chemo therapy session of Joshua. It's the total sum Angie was able to raise with the help of Donald, Anna and herself plus the people across their organization social media as medium of the fund-raising.

Robert went straight to his accommodation after having conversation with Donald. He has to prepare for his next training session with his coach – Jeff Gibbons.

Upon reaching their accommodation his room mates were having a party and drinking session in their room, which is pretty normal in Dubai after a long and busy day at work.

"Hey Robert join us here! Let's party all night long". Said one of his room mates.

"Thanks man, but I have to wake up early in the morning. I got an appointment to attend to." Robert replied.

"It's your lost. Good luck to you bro while we're having fun here". Answered back his room mates.

"It's alright guys just have fun ok!" Robert said.

It's very unusual for him to refuse a drink, especially during the time that he was very down. But somehow he has gained control of himself, if not the situation.

Upon hearing the prayer at a nearby mosque, which served to be his alarm ever since, he woke up and knelt down by the bed and prayed:

"Father God I thank you for taking care of me while I was asleep. Thank you for giving me another day to live. I commit into your hands the tasks that I'm supposed to do today. Keep my family safe back at home. Bless me all days of my life."

Robert arrived exactly at the right time and Jeff greeted him warmly.

"Hi Robert! I'm glad you made it on time this time". Jeff said.

"Yup, I'm happy I made it on time too for I don't wanna miss a lot of our training sessions". Robert replied.

"Now you're talking huh! At least we're arriving at something now. See time would be very much essential in our training, if not the most. As the saying goes: 'Time is gold', but I would say time is money, because I'm changing you free of charge". Jeff said.

"Thank you coach for your time and effort. I don't know how I can repay you for all of this". Robert told Jeff.

"Every time I see you Robert I can see myself through you for my own path of success. Just promise me one thing Robert when all of this is over". Jeff asked.

"Anything coach just tell me". Answered Robert.

"I'll tell it to you in the right time but for now let's get started and follow me in the track". Jeff instructed him.

"You bet coach". He replied.

Robert followed Jeff into the tracking field by the beach. And they started jogging along the 300-meters coast line, back and forth.

As they jog they continued their chat.

"So tell me Robert how was your whole week?" Asked Jeff.

"Oh it was good coach. I mean, I felt something different. Though the situation is still very tough. With my son's health condition and my relationship with my wife is falling apart plus the current status of my job, I felt inner peace when I followed your advice to attend church service and chat with my family". Robert explained.

"Glad to hear that. You know son to become successful means having a balance life. All of us came here in Dubai for a reason. Most of us though came for career and money, wether we admit it or not. Some came just to visit, see the beautiful city and have fun. Few even went here to escape from a predicament or from someone". Jeff said.

"That's very interesting, I never thought about it before". Answered Robert.

"If I may ask you Robert, why did you come here?" asked Jeff.

"Well, I guess I want to become successful just like everybody else. Otherwise, what am I here for?" replied Robert.

"Again all of us have a valid reason for being here. But for most of the people they see Dubai as a door of opportunity for success. Just like you are and there's absolutely nothing wrong with that. But you have to remember that true success means having a balance life. And having a balance life means not only you're successful in your career and finance. It also means having a healthy relationship with your family and having a strong personal relationship with your Creator".

"So last week I was rebuilding my relationship with my family and bonding with God. It makes sense now". Robert pondered.

"Now you are beginning to understand. What will your money and career do if you fail your relationship with your family? And worst if you forgot the One who gave you all of these blessings? Everything will fall apart Robert." Explained Jeff.

"Coach I think that's what exactly have happened to me…if I only knew". Robert told Jeff.

"Don't worry son, for as long as you commit to our training sessions and put it in your heart you can still re-claim the success that was once yours. Only this time, it's the true success". Jeff replied.

"Coach could we pause for a while? I feel the rush in my blood". Said Robert.

"C'mon son, don't tell me that I'm physically fitter than you. We have not reached the other end yet". Jeff teased Robert.

"I don't know each maybe I'm no longer use to this physical activities". Robert replied with his heartbeat running fast.

"Listen son, staying fit and healthy is a part of being successful. Especially here in Dubai, for people have no time to prepare their own food ending up in fast-food. Plus they got no time to exercise. So tell me what good is it to have lots of money if you end up being sick all the time and end up paying hospital bills and doctor's fee?" Jeff asked him.

"Off course it doesn't make sense to be wealthy but you're not healthy". Robert said.

"Exactly, because health is wealth". Jeff replied.

The two sat down on a bench to rest for few minutes then continued their exercise programme until 7 o'clock am.

Since then Robert managed to jog and exercise at least every other day even without his life coach around. He even quit his occasional smoking and drinking.

Another week had pass and Robert continued his training sessions. He felt peace and harmony in his life. Thanks for the effort of Jeff – his life coach and mentor. Though he knew he has still lots of mountains to conquer, Jeff gave him the right pathway and hope.

Until one day at work, as if Robert's faith and determination was really being tested. He received an SMS from his wife.

"Robert I don't want you to worry much about our son. For I know there are a lot things going through with you. But as the father of our son you deserve to know the truth and it's your right to know. The money that you sent to us three weeks ago was used for Joshua's chemo- therapy sessions. Until recently, his doctor told me that an immediate bone-marrow transplant operation is needed. Otherwise, his condition will be in critical. And the procedure alone will cost us almost half a million, and where in the world are we going to get that amount of money? Robert you told me to hold on and I'm holding on but I can't really take it whenever I see our boy suffering. Good thing he is a very jolly kid, he smiles always. But you can see in his eyes that he is in pain. Oh Robert, may God help us. I love you and we miss you…"

Robert wanted to burst into tears but he remained calm and composed. He remained silent for a few moments.

One of the staff approached him.

"Sir are you alright?"

"Yup. I'm totally fine". Robert answered.

Then he called on the shift leader to take charge because he wants to get some fresh air to breathe and to think. In his heart he wants to question the message of the 'One' above.

"Father in heaven, I know you're listening to me. And I know that you knew everything that is happening with my life, my family and my work. I know it's not your desire to put pain and sufferings to me especially to my son. But whatever your plan is, I submit into it. Help me understand the wisdom and the truth to all the details of my life and your plan for me. For I know you have great plans for me and not to harm me."

A few minutes after his quiet time, his phone rings. It's Jeff calling him.

> Robert: "Hi coach, glad to hear your voice."
>
> Jeff: "Same here Robert. I'm so excited to continue my training sessions with you".
>
> Robert: "Me too coach. And I think I really need to talk to you regarding my son, Joshua".

Jeff: "Ok we'll talk about when I come back. Listen, tomorrow we're not going to meet up but there is a task that I have assigned to you and you have to do it."

Robert: "What you mean?"

Jeff: "I have listed your name as a volunteer to one of Dubai's Charity Foundation. Don't worry everything has been arranged. All you have to do is show up yourself and look for Fatima. I'm pretty sure you're going to have fun and you'll learn a lot of things in that event."

Robert: "But coach you said it's a Charity Foundation and I myself needs some charity."

Jeff: "Oh son, don't be such a pity for yourself. Even if you don't have the resources to give, still you have a time and talent to share to someone in need. Just trust me on this one. So do I have your word?"

Robert: "Yes coach. I'll follow you instructions."

Jeff: "Good then. I'm going to send you an email for the details. And by the way tell to Fatima personally my warmest greetings when you meet her."

Robert checked his email and read Jeff's instructions. He was signed up by Jeff as a volunteer to Dubai helps. It's an organization founded by the Ruler of Dubai which main mission is to help deprived children of poor countries to have a better access to education, health and living.

After work Robert and Donald met at their favourite coffee shop near the Ice Rink area.

"I really don't see the wisdom why he wants me to work as a volunteer. In fact, I myself need some serious help financially and regarding my career. Especially now that my son is in a critical condition. Why should I bother myself to help other and the community?" Robert asked.

"Maybe your mentor is trying to teach you something". Donald replied.

"Well if there's any lesson that I want him to teach me is how can I able to produce one hundred thousand dirham in a limited period of time, to cover the cost of my son's operation." Robert said.

"Robert I just want you to know that you're like a brother to me. So whatever you need Anna and I are always here for you. But for now just follow the instructions of your mentor and maybe you'll find some answers to your problem". Donald told him.

"You better be right bro! thanks for the encouragement and I hope you'll meet Jeff in person". Robert smiled.

"Good luck bro and tell me you're adventure there ok?"

On the next day Robert went for leave and volunteered himself in Dubai Helps.

"Hi, good morning! My name is Robert and I'm looking for Fatima".

"Hello sir. Welcome to Dubai Helps! Are you one of the volunteers for today's activities?" the receptionist asked.

"Oh yes ma'am I'm a volunteer". He responded.

"Kindly fill up the registration here, then wait there at the lobby Ms. Fatima will be here in a few minutes". She said.

Robert filled up the registration then proceeded to the lobby. He sat down beside a woman who is holding a professional camera.

"Hi! I'm Robert. You have a nice camera. Are you also a volunteer? Or you work here?" Robert asked the woman.

"Yes. I'm also a volunteer. My name is Josie, I work as a nanny and photography is my hobby." She replied.

"Wow, I'm impressed by your character. I know you guys have a very little time to go out but still you managed to give your time to others for a worthy cause." Robert mentioned.

"So do you have any idea what's going to happen for the rest of the day?" Robert asked.

"Well, as for me my main task is to capture each moment while you guys are in action." She explained.

"Oh, that's wonderful. So you mean you are the official photographer for today's event?" he asked.

"Yes. I guess so, haha". She laughed.

"So how long you've been here in Dubai?" he asked.

"Actually, I'm about to end my 2$^{nd}$ year contract with my present employer. But they would not let me go to other employer until I pay them some amount of money. I think they're playing with me. It makes me worried but I'm here to help and enjoy." She answered.

"Ah I see, at least I'm pretty sure you're going to enjoy the event because you heart is here. Well as for me, I work in a Restaurant and I'm the manager but I'm about to loose my job in the coming months or weeks because of some mergers in our company. The hard part is, my son is in a serious health conditions and needs to be operated and here I am volunteering as per my mentor instructed me to do so." Robert pondered.

"Oh I'm sorry to hear that. But don't worry I'm sure at the end of the day somehow you will feel different after giving your time and effort and yourself to the people you barely know". She told him.

"Good day Ladies and Gentleman! My name is Fatima and I'm in charge for today's event. I would like to thank you all for showing up yourselves and sacrificing your time today. Your mere presence is a testimony that there are still individuals in today's environment that are not self-centered and are waiting to give back to the community their time, effort and talent. We need not your money because we already have huge donations from different sectors and groups. But more than money, we need people like you who has the heart and commitment to carry out our task, which is to provide quality eduation, healthy environment and provide better future for children who are less fortunate. Always remember that by helping others and helping them achieve their dreams you are also helping yourself to achieve yours".

"Today we are going to re-build a school for boys and girls in a remote area. We are going to re-build their school and their playground".

"So today to the eyes of the children you are their heroes. So if you're all ready for the action let's all hop in the bus and do some great deeds today". Fatima inspired them.

The volunteers worked hard the whole day. Some pointed the walls with beautiful decorations. Some fixed the windows and clean the classrooms. Others build new classrooms and playground. It's a team effort and they all gave their heart into it.

During their breaktime Robert received an SMS from Jeff:

"Hi Robert! I hope you're enjoying the activity. You might be wondering why I want you to volunteer in a community work. Perhaps, you know the answer now. Giving back to the community ourselves is one sign that we are on a right path to success. As you go up you let your feet stay on the ground. Always be grounded on the earth. And remember as you help other build and achieve their dreams you are also achieving yours it's called Infinite Networking. I don't want to bother you much so we'll see each other once I get back in the city. Don't forget to send my regards to Fatima. I'm proud of you." – Jeff G.

"Hey Robert this is my contact number so we'll keep in touch even after this event. Who knows? Maybe I can help your son in my own little way". Said Robin.

"Oh that's so kind of you, but I don't want to bother you much. I know your busy with your own problem". Replied Robert.

"I believe in the saying that whatever you do to the rest of the brethrens, you also do it to Him". Josie explained.

Then Robert remembered what his coach told him about helping people, the "Infinite Networking". He also gave Josie the contact details of his friend who works in Ministry of Labour and might help her case.

Their work has ceased before the sun set. Everyone was tired and exhausted but you can see the smile and joy in each and every faces of the volunteers.

Fatima personally thanked all the volunteers for their time, talent and effort.

"We look forward to seeing each and everyone of you in the next project of Dubai Helps." You are the very person that these children are given hope and future. So a big applause for all of you guys!" exclaimed Fatima.

And before they went back to their vehicle service, Robert approached Fatima to give the warm greetings of Jeff.

"Excuse me, Ms. Fatima I'm Robert and Jeff Gibbons is a good friend of mine. He wanted to send his warmest regards to you and to the whole team of your organization."

"Ah yes I remember Jeff. Off course when we started Dubai Helps couple of years ago he was one of few guys who generously gave his support to us. Both in finances and time. And the last time I've heard about him was that he set up his own firm and became very successful in his field." Said Fatima.

"That's true Ms. Fatima. As a matter of fact, he's the one who encouraged me to become a volunteer of this organization." Robert said.

"That's good to know. Tell him I wish him more success and if he needs anything we're always here to help him". She replied.

"Surely I'll pass on the message". He told her.

It was indeed a long day and tiring for the volunteers but you can see all the smiles in them. Robert for the meantime has forgotten his own problems while giving his time, talent and effort.

And during the night before Robert closed his eyes he prayed:

"Father God in heaven I thank you for blessing my life with my family, friends and for giving me the chance to help others despite my short-comings and my own afflictions in life. I'm praying that you may reveal your plan for me as I seek you. As my son lays down in bed may you touch his life and heal him in his sickness. And whatever your will is let it be done. Amen."

He received and SMS from Jeff very early in the morning.

"Good day Robert! Meet me today to the World Trade 9am. There is something I want to show you".

So Robert called up to his co-manager to tell that his coming in the afternoon shift.

Robert prepared himself for he know that Jeff will give him a new lesson to become a true success.

He took the METRO which goes directly at the World Trade.

Upon entering the main hall he was greeted by his coach, Jeff.

"Hi Robert, how you do?" greeted Jeff.

"I'm fine and excited for today's session". Answered Robert.

"Indeed. I'm going to show you something that will, I hope, change your belief and view about money". Explained Jeff.

"Wow! I'm so excited. Can we begin?" asked Robert.

"Come follow me". Said Jeff.

And the two walked continuously to the other end of the building until they reached the entry of Dubai Financial Market.

"Where are we coach?" asked Robert.

"We are at the heart of the trading business. Particularly, 'Stock Market'." Jeff told him.

The electronic board hanging up and showing different company names and their stock quotes caught Robert's attention.

"And what these things have to do with our session?" Robert seems confused.

"A lot Robert. You told me before that you want to get ahead financially and that's one reason you came here in Dubai am I right?" Jeff asked him.

"Yes. You are definitely right coach." Answered Robert.

"So you think for a while…how much you think is enough for your retirement fund? We're talking about long term here". Jeff questioned him again.

"I'm not sure coach. Maybe a quarter of a million dirham or half a million." Answered Robert.

"C'mon Robert, don't be shy. This is your chance to declare what you want. No one will stop you. But just be specific, it should be measurable, attainable, realistic and time-bounded." Explained Jeff.

"Ok. I declare to have at least a million dirham in my account in order for me to pay for my son's surgery. And to help other people as well." Robert pondered.

"I'm impressed. But do you think that by simply working as an employee will help you reach your financial goal?" Jeff asked.

"Well I worked hard and I can prove that. When I came here I was just a crew and now I'm the manager…who is about to loose his job the coming days." Sighed Robert.

"That is exactly why we are here. See Robert in order to get ahead financially, yes you need to work hard. But you also need to work smart and leverage yourself. You have to create a money machine that will put money into your pocket automatically." Jeff told him.

"Huh? And how would I do that?" Robert asked.

"Look, actually your labour and your body is already a money machine but only it's in manual. If you work you get paid, if you don't get up in your bed and log in to your office you also don't get paid. It's as simple as that."

"Yeah. That sounds fair and square." Robert agreed.

"However, if you have an automatic money machine such as stocks, bonds, or other paper investments and businesses or real estate properties even royalties, then it will come automatically to your pocket though you're sitting at your home-desk." Jeff explained.

"Now coach you're telling things that I'm not aware before. All I know was to work hard and save money in the bank. Or like before, I just work and spend and enjoy the money that I have." Robert pondered.

"Don't worry Robert that's why we're here to break that habit and belief. Remember, that a habit or thought are a thousand time more powerful than desires or decisions."

"See Robert, the people who have investment in the stocks gain money higher than when they put their money in the bank for as long as they know what they are doing."

"Again Robert, I'm not saying that you put all you money in the stocks or whatever investments are available out there. Every investment or business decisions need to have a careful planning and exit strategy."

Remember, that a habit or thought are a thousand time more powerful than desires or decisions."

"Oh I see. I actually thought of not waiting the management decision if they will extend me and just go home and invest or set up my own business." Robert said.

"My son listen – I brought you here so that your mind and thoughts will be open about business and investing so you can get ahead financially. But it does not mean you quit your day job and resigned right away. What you can do is keep your day job and start investing or have a business on the side." Jeff explained further.

"That's a good advice coach." Robert replied.

"Remember to start small but think big. Great people started with a humble beginning." Jeff said.

"Amazing coach you taught me a lot. So I want to start now!" Robert eagerly told Jeff.

"Patience my son. Financial wealth is not a quick-rich scheme. It cannot be accumulated over-night. It needs determination and discipline." Jeff further explained.

"But coach you don't understand…I needed the money now for my son's operation as quickly as possible and I entails a huge amount of money." Robert argued.

"Slow down my son, you look worried. I'm sorry to hear about your son. Remember what I told you – just do everything you can and leave it all up to Him." Jeff suggested.

"Coach, can't you just lend me the money? And I'm sure I'll find ways to pay you back." Robert said.

"And how much are we talking about?" asked Jeff.

"A hundred thousand dirham maybe, more or less." Robert replied.

"And how much time is left?" Jeff inquired.

"My wife said the doctors told her that the operation should take place within 2 weeks". Robert replied

"Even I lend you the money it would take me more than two weeks to produce that amount." Jeff said.

"Coach I got an idea!" Robert exclaimed.

"And what is that?" Jeff asked.

"You told me that this training session we are having right now will cost you around 500dhs. And you are giving it in small group because you want it to be exclusive right?" Robert said.

"Yes. That is right because I want my delegates to feel that what they paid for is only for exclusive members, so they feel important and privileged." Jeff replied.

"Coach, I'm thinking of launching a huge seminar and you will do exactly as what we are doing now. Also, it would take you to the next level." Robert challenged him.

"Ok. That sounds good. But say we are able to register a huge number of people, getting that amount in a limited time is quite challenging. There are other factors that we have to consider like instalment payments, those who will pay by credit card and getting the proper venue for the event, and a lot more." Jeff sounded pessimistic.

"But it's not impossible. You're the one who told me that we should do our part and let God do the rest." Robert said.

"I can see in you the determination and the fire in your heart. I also had a mentor before who said that a size of the result determines the size of the answer. And you have a big answer that needs a big result. Alright. Let's do it!" Jeff shouted.

"Thank you coach!" Robert tears started to fall.

"We have to act fast but every move shall be carefully planned. It's impossible to do this task just the two of us. So we need to make a team." Jeff told him.

"I think I can help you with that. I have three friends whom I trust and believe are willing to part of this challenge." Robert said.

"Ok. Try to talk to them and we'll set a meeting as soon as possible. I will contact you 24/7. I will also try to call my business partners if they can finance the money or at least half, in case anything goes wrong." Jeff explained.

"I don't know how can I repay you for everything, coach." Robert said.

"Don't mention it. I believe you are also going to do it if we are on each other's shoes. But there's one more thing I want you to do. A day after tomorrow there is a Dubai Money Boot Camp. It's a seminar about Investing and Finance and I want you to be there. You might get an idea, just open your mind. Feed your hunger and always look fool." Jeff instructed him.

"Coach, do I really need to attend it? I think I've had enough with you." Robert asked.

"My son remember this: 'Your character is built by the people you associate with, the books that you read and the seminar you attend to'." Jeff said.

And that ended their day session. Robert went straight to his workplace and Jeff contacted his business partner who can finance the money needed.

The question is – given the limited period of time can they produce that huge number of participants for the seminar? Is less than two weeks enough for them to prepare everything? Can they produce hundred thousand dirham in a short period of time? And a lot more questions...

Meanwhile, Robert made up his team.

He contacted his best friend Donald. Donald included his fiance' Anna in the team. And lastly, Angie volunteered to be a part of the team. She learned everything through Donald.

Robert made a phone call to Jeff.

Robert: "Coach I have a good news!"

Jeff: "Whoah...you sound so excited. Tell me.

Robert: "My team is now complete to do the challenge. I know we don't have that much time but we are all very positive and determined."

Jeff: "Listen, let's meet up at the Burj Al Arab Lounge. It's the only 7-star hotel in the world. And it's a good place to make our 'gameplan'."

Robert: "That would be a real pleasurable experience coach."

Jeff: "Indeed. I have already made a reservation, just send me their names. I will send a driver to pick you up.

Robert: "See you then."

After work, Robert together with Angie, Donald and Anna went straight to Burj. They were picked up by Jeff's driver.

As they arrived at the entrance gate they were checked by the security and confirmed their reservation.

Everyone was amazed by their dramatic entrance to the Burj while crossing the bridge.

The group entered the hotel and seated at lobby. They were mesmerized by the elegant interior design (made for royalties) with gold all over the place. Plus the huge aquarium on both sides of the lobby complement the whole thing.

"I have lived here in Dubai for a few years but it's my first time to enter here. For me everything is normal when you're inside." Anna commented.

"It seems our meeting tonight is very much important and high-profile." Donald shared.

"Well as for me, I just want to help you Robert. After all of this is done. We can all go home and live our own lives." Angie said.

"Guys, all I can say is thank you all for the support and for showing up here tonight. Rest be assured that your life will never be the same again once we completed our task; and we'll all share the fruits of our labour." Robert told everyone.

"Robert what are you saying? We all showed up because we care for you and we are your friend. We are willing to help without any exchange at all." Donald sighed.

"I made no mistake in selecting my 'dream team!'" Robert exclaimed

"You bet!" – everyone shouted.

A few minutes later, Jeff arrived and he waved at the group. They went to the Hotel's Restaurant which serves all kinds of International Cuisine – Mediterranean, Continental, Asian, etc.

"Ladies and Gentleman, before we proceed to our agenda let us loosen up a bit. I know you're tired and it was a long day. So let's proceed to the buffet table and fill up our hungry stomach." Jeff invited them

"Remember you can have everything you want from starter up to the main dish and even all kinds of desserts."

After saying that nobody was moving from their seats and everyone was looking at each other.

"Hey didn't you hear me guys?" Jeff asked.

"Umm…Coach we didn't expect that we are going to have a buffet dinner here…and we know that it might not reach our budget." Robert explained.

"C'mon guys!" feel free. Don't worry about the bill, I'll take care of it. What's the use of being here in the most luxurious hotel in the world if we're not going to savor every bit of it." Jeff told everyone.

So everyone went ahead and took their meal.

They had everything – from seafood to pasta and caviar plus all varieties of dessert. It was a truly an engulfing and rich experience.

After they have tasted almost everything Jeff said his piece.

"Guys, I'm really glad to see you all here. Maybe Robert had share with you that for a couple of weeks I've been mentoring him on how to be successful in his life – in all areas. And I also knew the current situation of his life. But, as we are about to go to our final mentoring session, something came up which would really test everything he has learned. And to top it all, we should be able to produce a huge amount of money in a short period of time – to save the life of his son." Jeff explained.

"Excuse me Sir or if I may also call you coach, I believe we're all here to give our help and support to our good friend here. So just tell us exactly what we need to do so we can start." Donald butt in.

"By the way, do we really have to do our meeting here?" Angie asked.

"Guys, I really admire your support and the positivity I can feel in each and everyone of you. First of all, let me tell you that this would not be an easy task. Given the odds, we have a little chance of getting our target: 100,00 dhs in less than two weeks. But my mentor also has told me once that with the right people and a right goal, everything is possible."

"And to answer your question why we are meeting up here, that is exactly the point. I want you all to feel empowered, and feel motivated to have that burning desire to reach our goal."

"Also, I have noticed that you were bit hesitant when I said we are about to dine. Is it because you have not yet internalized that you are about to eat in the most expensive hotel in the world?"

Everyone remained silent.

"Let me tell you this: "Unless you have increase your 'intellectual wallet' the amount that we are targeting cannot go into your 'physical wallet'. And as we fill our 'physical wallet', a 'spiritual wallet' will finally be our break-through." Jeff said.

"Wow! I'm learning something I have not known before." Anna said.

"And as you go along with this task you will learn a lot more. Remember, you have to fail your way to success. But given the limited time as we will use other people's experience, time and money to reach our goal." Jeff pondered.

"And if we fail?" Angie asked.

"Then fail some more...Failure is our best teacher because it's the first step towards success."

"But coach, how can we fail if our time is so limited?" Donald asked.

"That's why you have to learn from it and next time you know what to do or not to do." Jeff answered.

"Robert can you enlighten the team about you idea?" Jeff instructed him.

"Before I share it, everyone may feel free to give their thoughts, comments or feedbacks. We are one team now.

Everyone nodded their heads.

"Alright here's the plan – since Mr. Jeff Gibbons is a life coach and has been mentoring individuals and professionals on a one on one basis and the most would be a private class in a group of 6-12 persons; I have come up with an idea of holding a huge seminar." Robert suggested.

"And what seminar are we talking about?" Angie asked.

"Seminar about 'success' and Jeff Gibbons would be the guest speaker. And we're talking about a crowd of 500 people or more." Robert answered.

"How about the fee? How much are we going to charge them?" Anna asked.

"Well let's ask coach here: Coach how much usually do you charge your client for one session?" Robert asked him.

"It depends. If for example it's a one on one session, I charge my client 150AED to 200AED." Jeff told him

"And how long is the session?" Robert ask again

"Two hours approximately. For my class session composed of 6-12 persons, I normally charge them 100AED-150AED." Jeff said.

"How much are we targeting again?" Donald asked.

"One hundred thousand dirhams in less than 2 weeks!" exclaimed Robert.

"Oh boy that's a real challenge!" Anna pondered.

"We can also try to divide it in separate days because surely it would be exhausting to talk to a hundred of people for a couple of hours." Angie suggested.

"Or we can also hire other motivational speakers so that we divide it in separate sessions." Donald said.

"Team, listen, all of you have a nice idea. However, since our time is limited I think it's best to split the teams into two groups. Agree?" Jeff asked everyone.

"Agree!" – everyone responded.

"Robert and Angie you're going to team up. You're main task is to invite as many participants as you can. If you can get a thousand invitees, it's much better. Remember this is a number game. Even if you get a thousand prospects most likely only half will confirm or even less." – Jeff told them

"But coach how about the programme? Who will do it?" Robert asked.

"Don't worry about the programme I have my own staff who'll take care of that." Jeff told him.

"Getting a huge crowd is not a problem. We can use social media and we'll tap into large groups and organizations. As long as the programme is excellent and they will surely benefit from it, registration fee is not a problem." Angie said.

"Well said. Now, Donald and Anna, both of you will try to look for motivational speakers or those individuals who are already successful in different fields such as career, health, business and investing, personal finance, spiritual leaders even philanthropist. We will partner with them." Jeff explained.

"Whew! I'm really excited to meet those type of persons. But where in the world we'll find them?" – Donald sighed.

"Don't worry, I have list here of people whom I've dealt before of partnered with. So I'm going to leave you the task of contacting them. But also you have to be resourceful, search online, look in the ads or newspaper. Use everything, exhaust all you resources." – Jeff said.

"I just have one question…What are we going to call the seminar?" Anna addressed the group.

"Good question. Since every minute is counting as we speak and we have a target time. We will name the seminar – One

Minute Dubai – how to 'mind map' you way to success. And in fact, I'm going to call you group: One Minute Dubai." Any violent reactions?" – Jeff asked.

And all of them gave their two thumbs up.

On that same night their team was established – One Minute Dubai. And their mission is to produce at least one hundred thousand dirhams in less than two weeks by holding a seminar.

Everyone filed for a leave at their respective work so at least they can concentrate on their project.

Jeff instructed the team to attend a Money Boot Camp Seminar before they officially begin their task.

So the team composed of Robert, Donald, Angie and Anna attended the seminar as per Jeff's instruction.

"Why do we need to attend this? Can we just proceed to our task?" Angie asked.

"Surely, we'll get some ideas here. Otherwise, coach would not let us waste our time here." Robert replied.

After the registration the seminar started.

"Ladies and Gentlemen welcome to the Annual Dubai Money Boot Camp. I'm Edward Ramos your speaker for today's seminar. It's our mission to raise financial education to each and everyone living in this country and to open you eyes to the investment opportunities that are available in the market. As you all know we are all working and living here just for temporary and one day we're all going back to our home countries. And we don't want to ask ourselves: where did we put all our money after all those years of hard work? So I hope you'll have a wonderful experience today and just try to open your mind and offcourse have fun!"

"But before the actual seminar we're going to play first." The speaker said.

"Excuse me sir, we went here to learn and not to play." Angie reacted.

"Exactly that's the point. You are all here to learn while you play." Answered the speaker.

"Wow! Can we start. I'm getting excited." Donald exclaimed.

"Ok. We are going to divide you in a group of six. Each group will be given a game board. But it's not an ordinary game board, it's a money game board, created by a genius entrepreneur." Speaker said.

"So it's like the game board, Monopoly." One participant said.

"Well in a way yes, but it's much more different. Each player will have a chance to pick a career. From there the game would start. As the game progress you'll be given a chance to invest in small and big deals like bonds, mutual fund, stock market, real estate and business."

"Sounds like a complicated game huh!" – one participant commented.

"Actually the game is only a reflection of how well you do in your actual financial life and decisions in life. And you are able to partner yourself with other player or you can study their strategy. So it's also relationship game you can say." The speaker said.

"And how are we going to win?" – asked by one of the participant.

"Good question. Remember, you are all given a particular career like a doctor, lawyer, teacher, nurse, fireman, etc. There is a high-paying job and the middle income one. But it's not a matter who earns more it's a matter of who keeps more and invest in business or other investment vehicles. Your goal is to get out of the 'life's maze' and achieve 'financial freedom'.

"So you mean to say we might play as a high paid professional and still end up in 'life's maze' as you call it." Asked by one of the participant.

"Exactly true. And it also happens in real life"

"So what are we waiting for?...let's get started" Robert suggested.

The game started and Robert, Angie, Donald and Anna played in the same game board along with other participants.

The people who attended the Annual Dubai Money Boot Camp came from different walks of life – architects, engineers, doctors, shop crew, sales executive, banker, even students and a few businessmen.

As the game progressed excitement and hype were on a high level. There were players who accumulated tons of money then at one point, lost everything in one stock market crash.

Some started slowly but after investing in few solid real estate their assets paid them huge income so they bought more investments.

A lot of them borrowed money in the bank to cover their monthly expenses and ended up in deep debt. Though some used the bank to finance small and big business deals.

And there was a guy who ended up giving almost all of his assets is generating much more over his expenses. And he's the one who finished the game first.

After one hour of fun and excitement the organizers called to end the game due to time constraint. Though the players were eager to finish the game.

All the participants were gathered in-front and they started the seminar.

"I really hope you did enjoy the game." Asked the speaker.

And everyone started laughing and sharing their own experience.

"Listen everyone, the way you played in the game is exactly the same way you deal with your own life. If you ended up in big debt most likely you are doing the same thing in your life right now."

"Sir I just came to realize how bad I am when it comes to finances and decisions" – participant commented.

"Like what I told you the game is only a reflection of who you are. But the good news is that it's just a game and you can still make a change in your life. That is why we're all here." So give yourselves a big applause for being here."

And a barrage of applause was heard all over the seminar hall.

"Ladies and Gentlemen let me show you a glimpse of my life for the past 20 years of investing.

And a video clip was played showing how his life was completely changed by doing the business and investing.

*"When I was still a small child I was told by my wealthy step Dad that if I wanted to be like him I should never work for the money.*

*On the other hand my real and poor dad used to tell me that I should work very hard for the money by getting a high paying job or career after graduation.*

*The irony is my wealthy Dad who owns business and a lot of investments had never been to a formal school and not even reached secondary level. And my poor Dad is a Phd.*

*When they both died this was the realization that opened my mind: My wealthy Dad left a legacy of businesses and investment and touching the lives of many. While my highly educated Dad died unemployed and left a will of debts."*

"All of us have a salary whether huge or small. But the secret to become financially wealthy is to convert your salary to a passive income. Where your money will work for you and not you working for the money." Speaker addressed.

"But how is that?" one teacher asked.

"Its is said that the greatest magic in the world is...compound interest. My dear friends make it your ally and not your enemy. So when you hear all those enticing offeres: no money down, low interest rate, etc. don't believe the hype because as time passes by compound interest will kill you." the speaker explained.

"Sir can you explain it further?" one lady asked.

"Remember this – in the world of finance and money there are only three types of a person: spender, saver, and investor. The question is: which one are you?" – the speaker threw a question.

And everyone looked at each other.

"A spender is the one who works hard all year round and spends all his money to treat himself, his family and friends. Whereas, the saver also works hard whole year round and put all his money in the bank. And I pity the savers, because of the term called 'inflation'. They don't realize that their money looses its value while sleeping in the bank. Lastly, we have the investors. They are the people who also works hard but they are also smart because they put their hard earned money in an investment vehicles like mutual fund, bonds, stock market, real estate, or business. And most often than not, they are the one who have planned for their retirement life."

"Whew! These terms are new to me all I know is to put my money in the bank." One guy exclaimed.

"No offense to all the bankers right here. Bank can help you a lot especially in financing business deals like what I do. But sorry to say that bank is not the right path to put your money in a long-term."

And the people's faces looked blank to what the speaker had said.

"I can understand if what I'm saying looks strange to you but let me show you a graph to have a better understanding."

"But before I show it, does anyone here have 50AED?" asked the speaker.

And plenty of people raised their hands.

"Do you believe that 50AED lies 50 AED millions?"

Everyone looked stunned.

"Let me show this graph:"

| | Put it under your bed forever. | Bank (time deposit 3%/year) | Rural Islamic Bank 5%/year |
|---|---|---|---|
| 50 Dhs. | 50 Dhs. (still the same) | 50 Dhs. Million (468 years) | 50 Dhs. Million (284 years) |

| | Govt. Bonds, (10%) Retail treasury | Equity Fund 15% years (bonds, stock) |
|---|---|---|
| 50 Dhs. | 50 Dhs. Million (145 years) | 50 Dhs. Million (99 years) |

"So Ladies and Gentlemen, it is very clear that even your 1 dirham a day can grow 1 million dirham in the right investment vehicle. You can either walk, take a bicycle, ride a motor vehicle, or even ride on a plane. But why walk when you can fly?" the speaker explained.

Now I have a bonus for you today. Who puts all of their savings in the bank?

And almost one third of the crowd raised their hand.

Good job! Says the speaker. He continued speaking: Listen I have nothing against the bank if there are bankers here thank you, because you have been my partner in my business ventures and for financing my projects

And the crowd was awaiting for his next punch line...

But people, you must understand that there are other investment vehicles that are far more generous in making your money work hard for you aside from the traditional bank.

Can you show us please? One guy asked.

Okay. Let me ask you, what much percentage doe syour bank gives interest to our money? Say 2% per year.

Not even close! Its only 1% in my bank. A lady shouted.

Exactly, that's the point here. But do you think that your bank invest your money where it will yield 1 or 2% or even 5%? I don't think so ladies & gentlemen. You're bank put you r money in an investment where it will yield a much higher interest like in loans, real estate, stocks, mutual funds, business acquisitions, etc. And in return they will give you only a portion of a pie. And that is your hard earned money. And seemingly your money does not work hard for you but work hard for the bank.

And the crowd began to talk to each other, looking stunned by the information given by the speaker.

But we're still little confused, so how and where then should we invest our money if not in the bank. – the people asked.

I will reveal to you what my financial mentor taught me, it's the Rule of 72.

And what is the Rule of 72? An old guy asked

Now the whole crowd gives their full attention

The 'Rule of 72' is a simplified way to determine how long an investment will take to double, given a fixed annual rate of interest. By dividing 72 by the annual rate of return, investors can get a rough estimate of how many years it will take for the initial investment to duplicate itself.

For example, the rule of 72 states that 1 AED invested at 10% would take 7.2 years ((72/10) = 7.2) to turn into 2 AED. In reality, a 10% investment will take 7.3 years to double ((1.10^7.3 = 2).

And he showed them a graph to make it easier.

| Rate of Return | Rule of 72 | Actual # of Years | Difference (#) of Years |
|---|---|---|---|
| 2% | 36.0 | 35 | 1.0 |
| 3% | 24.0 | 23.45 | 0.6 |
| 5% | 14.4 | 14.21 | 0.2 |
| 7% | 10.3 | 10.24 | 0.0 |
| 9% | 8.0 | 8.04 | 0.0 |
| 12% | 6.0 | 6.12 | 0.1 |
| 25% | 2.9 | 3.11 | 0.2 |
| 50% | 1.4 | 1.71 | 0.3 |
| 72% | 1.0 | 1.28 | 0.3 |
| 100% | 0.7 | 1 | 0.3 |

"Excuse me sir, how can we start investing if money is our problem?" one gentlemen asked.

And everyone in the hall nodded.

"Honestly sir I don't believe that money is the problem. It's just a symptom. We have to dig deeper. Maybe its your lifestyle, spending habits or even the way you budget your money." The speaker said.

"Let me tell you a secret."

"I have always kept myself from acquiring bad debts which takes away money from my pocket; rather I always keep good debt which puts money in my pocket. And when you receive your salary, here's how you should budget it: Live 70% of your income. And set aside 30% of your income for the 4 special funds."

"They are:"

1. Freedom fund – 6.66% of income to pay in advance your debt;
2. Emergency fund – 6.66% of your income to be put in the bank until it reaches 3-6 months of your salary;
3. Wealth fund – 6.66% of your income but if you are finished with Freedom and Emergency Fund you are to put 20% of your income to wealth fund;
4. Tithe fund – 10% of your income you give to God and you income will multiply.

"How can we join a Networking Business or have our part-time business if we are tied up to our work and we only have few time left to rest?" said one of the attendees.

"Remember that there are only two things you can invest in – time and money. If you invest in money then you loose both.

"Have you ever heard an employee who became rich because of his job? The reality is that you are making the owners of the company you're working for richer."

"Yes, we're all working here as an expat but should have a plan B in case you want to go home, got fired, or resigned." The speaker said.

"As I end my talk let me say that your present is my past and my present is your future. Everything is in you hands now so you make a choice to change your life. See you all on top." Edward added.

"After the talk those who are interested in the investment programs and advanced trainings of the Money Boot Camp were assessed by the volunteers."

The group of Robert stayed and they were given a financial check up. A financial check up is like having a body x-ray. It shows which area of your financial life needs to be diagnosed and treated.

After the seminar, Robert personally talked to Edward, the speaker, if he can be his financial and business mentor since Robert was motivated by Edward's testimony.

He told Edward about the challenge that he and his group are about to accomplish.

Edward told them that their investment programs would require ample time before they can get the amount needed.

However, he also advised the group that they can by something else, which will involve risk. But not trying at all is also a risk. The fact that a life is at stake, so what is there to loose?

"What you can do is get a flat or one whole villa then make a rent out of it." Edward suggested.

"And how much money we can earn from it?" Robert asked.

"Well it depends on how many tenants you can get and wether you charge them per room or per person. Say for example you get a flat (3bedrooms) in a building and you lease it for 30,000/year, if you can fill each room 4-6 persons and you charge them 600 per person. It means your potential income is around 8000 Dhs." Edgar explained.

"Well, we're still short of 92000 Dhs. to reach our target. But it would help." Donald said.

"And what they require for us to get a flat?"

"It's just a cheque. And your persistently to get a tenant. You should entice them with benefits like Wi-fi, cable, pool and gym etc. But given a very short period of time, it would be very difficult." Edward told the group.

"Like I told you sir, there's nothing to loose." Robert replied.

"Well, all I can say is good luck to all of you and all the best. See you all on top" Edward said.

Robert gathered his group.

"Guys, slight change of plan. Still, we're going to get as much as participant as we could for our One Minute Dubai seminar. But as we proceed with our separate task we're also going to find a good place where we could lease either a flat or villa then we'll advertise on the newspaper." Robert suggested.

"Would it not interfere with our original task? Besides, assuming that we found a good location, where are we going to get the cheque? And maybe there will be some reservation needed." Anna sighed.

"Like I said our main task is still our own seminar. Me and Angie will get as many prospects as we can. Along our search if we find any good place for leasing property then we'll let you know. And you also do the same thing. While looking for the possible speakers to be our partner, if you see any location that looks profitable for leasing business let us know. I'm going to talk to Jeff if he can issue a cheque just in case." Robert said.

"Alright then let's do it!" Donald replied.

"Guys before we leave this area don't you notice that we are in the right area for our main goal?" Angie asked everyone.

"What you mean?" Robert answered.

"Are we not in a seminar and there are a lot of people whom we can invite as well in our own seminar. And I'm sure that the organizers of this event have a huge database and we'll just have to talk to them." Angie suggested."

"That is if they are willing to give it." Anna challenged her.

"For sure there's a way. If we can convince them that they would also benefit from it, it think it's possible." Robert countered.

"Let me do it guys. I'll try to use my charisma." Angie said.

So Angie went ahead to the organizers of the event. She was told to speak to the president of the organization. And luckily he didn't leave yet the hall.

The group had a view from a distance how Angie and the gentleman converse with each other. A few gestures…body language…and a lot of smile and confidence from Angie.

The group were crossing all their fingers…

A couple of minutes after, Angie looked back to them and gave her two thumb's up.

And the group rejoiced.

They were given a copy of the seminar's database. It's about three thousand prospects, more than what they needed.

"Angie, can you tell us how did you convince that guy to give that info?" Robert wondered.

"Well, first I have introduced myself and our group. Then I told him about the seminar that we are planning to host next week and we need people who will register for it." Angie said.

"Is that it?" Donald asked.

"Then he asked me if we can talk about formally in a business dinner. Angie replied.

"Then you said yes." Robert said.

"Not exactly. But I told him that I will tell my boss about it. And when he asked who's my boss, I told him his Jeff Gibbons. Then he was surprised. He told me that Jeff has helped his organization grow when it was just starting. So by all means he is willing to return the favour to Jeff by all means." Angie explained.

"Oh really. We're not expecting that." Anna told her.

"Truly, Jeff has helped a lot of people. It's what he called 'Infinite Networking' and it has a good ripple effect." Robert told everyone.

"So guys, I think we have to split up. Anna and I will now proceed with our task and we shall contact you soon." Donald said.

"Okay, let's split up then. Any developments or updates just contact us." Robert replied.

The group split up after the seminar and they told Jeff about the recent plan and what occurred in the seminar.

Jeff congratulates the team for their first achievement and told them it's a long way to go.

Robert and Angie went to an internet café to start the selecting process. They have sent invitation of the One Minute Dubai Seminar to the emails they got from Money Boot Camp Seminar. Some are active and are dummies and no longer working.

They also initialized the social media network like facebook, Twitter and youtube in sending of the invitation to make it more powerful and robust.

A video presentation about the seminar was also attached in the invitation

After spending the whole afternoon at the internet café they went straight to Media City for advertisement.

It was bit difficult for them to talk to the people in Media City.

Fortunately, when they mentioned the name Jeff Gibbons in their inquiry, one guy knew him well. This guy worked as a PR for a lot of news and media company. And this time he has established his own firm through the help of Jeff Gibbons.

"Guys my name is Richard. I have been a PR for a long time, and my dream is to have a PR firm of my own. I've met Jeff in one of my projects. Actually he had been not only as a colleague but a good friend and advisor as well". He said.

So by all means you'll have my support. I'll use my contact and resources to help you" Richard added.

'Oh that would be so great sir. Mr. Jeff Gibbons was so happy to hear about you'. Robert told him.

'All pleasure is mine. tell him to visit me in my place. It's been a long time a long time since we last seen each other'. Richard said.

'Surely, we'll let him know' Angie noted.

Meanwhile, while Donald and Anna were driving along business bay metro station, they found a new building and they are leasing tenants.

Since the occupancy rate is low, the realtor is giving it in an introductory offer. It's a 3 bedroom flat with amenities like pool and gym.

However, there's a little problem. They are asking 1 month advance and 1 month deposit amounting to almost five thousand dirham. But where would they get such amount?

They made a phone call to Robert.

"hi Robert, guess what, we found a nice leasing property somewhere in Business Bay, It fits the description that we wanted, One thing though there's an advance and deposit. We need to produce five thousand dirham. 'believe we can really make a profit if we can fill it up with tenants.' Robert explained

'That's a good news'. Good job guys! Tell them we're interested.

Robert answered.

'How about the money needed? Where we are going to get it? Donald asked.

'Don't worry about it. I'll talk to Jeff if he can help us with that amount. Meanwhile, proceed with the original plan. Keep on looking for motivational speakers, surely our seminar will be a huge one and we need additional speakers.

Robert told him.

'alright copy that bro' sees you soon. Bye! – Donald said.

Robert immediately called Jeff regarding the group's plan of leasing a property and makes a profit from it by looking for tenants. Jeff replied objectively to their plan and asked for a group meeting at his place.

It's almost midnight when the group arrived at their respective homes.

'Angie thank you for everything and I hope you have forgiven me'. Robert look straight in her eyes.

I have already forgiven you. I am doing this to payback the good deeds you have shown me. You made me strong and you built my character. Also, I want you to be reunited with your family and I really would do anything for the recovery of your son.' Angie said.

'I'm glad to know that you, Donald and Anna are there for my family. I'll cherish you guys until the final breathe of my life. Robert sighed.

'Now, you're being sentimental… I think we have to go home because we'll meet Jeff early in the morning. 'Angie commented.

'If you will allow me take you in a cab'. Robert asked.

'Surely, so drop me first then we'll see each other in the morning'. Angie said.

For Donald and Anna, the task given to them to look for other speakers and along the way they found a nice flat where they can profit is an adventure on their relationship.

It was a nice bonding moment for them, plus it added a little spice into their relationship because they are also a part of the One minute Dubai challenge which involves a matter of life and death.

'Donald, do you really think that we can produce that amount of money'? Anna questioned him.

'You mean you're doubling our mission? Donald ask her.

'Off course not. But I'm just thinking what if it there would be problems or delays along the way. I'm sure the surgery operation could not wait any longer'. Anna replied.

'Well in that case only God knows', because even me I don't know what will happen next. Let's just do our part and cross our fingers', Donald answered back.

'See you tomorrow then goodnight'. Anna said

Goodnight too. Take your rest because tomorrow will be another long day for ll of us'. Donald told her.

And they kissed each other as they parted.

While in bed, Robert had his quiet time for himself and for his creator. He thanks him for the developments of their mission and he asked for all the blessings of their team.

As he went into sleep he had vision a dream...

In a dream he was holding a gentle lamb that got sick. But after few moments the gentle lamb died in his hands. He was deeply saddened by the loss of his lamb. And when he opened a door he was surprised to see a multitude of lamb and he cared of all of them and gave them a shelter.

When he woke up he prayed fervently about his dream. For even himself he does not have any idea what is it all about.

It's already 6 o'clock in the morning. He get up put on his running shoes and went for a jogging and exercise along the beach. He meditated and released all the tension and pressure his group is having.

At exactly 9 am all of them gathered at Jeff's place to give reports and updates of the situation.

'Good morning to all of you! First let me congratulate your group for the fast developments in our One Minute Dubai project.

You all deserve a big applause. Jeff said

And the meeting room was filled with claps and praises.

'ok now both teams will report to give us the updates. Let's start with Robert and Angie'. Jeff Instructed them.

'So far so good. We have sent out invites to almost four thousand people.

Three thousand came from the visit of Dubai Money Boot Camp and the rest came from the network of Angie and me. We have also use the social media as a tool of communication. Plus of course the word of mouth help a lot'. Robert explained.

'And how many delegates are we targeting to reach our goal' Jeff asked.

'Well it depends on how much are we going to charge them. On the invitation no amount was mentioned. So when they reply or inquire about it then we are going to tell the amount'. Angie replied

'Actually, I'm thinking of doing something different with our seminar. I want the delegates to feel very special and to have a very rich experience. Just like the you had at the Burj, so thinking of charging them around 500 dirhams, But half of that will cover the cost of the place'. Jeff explained.

'if that's the case then we need approximately 400 delegates. Because if per delegate would pay 500 dirhams half of that will cover the expense, that would leave us with 250 dirhams, and to achieve our target which is 100,000 dirhams we need around 400 delegates. Anna said.

'Good analysis katie'. Donald commented.

'Alright let's all wait for the confirmation of the delegates then we'll decide on it'. Jeff said.

'Now let's carry on. Donald and Anna can you tell us any development on your side. Jeff added.

'Well we have talked to a few number of motivational speaker here in Dubai. No one has confirmed yet but we are to follow up on them. I think if we are going to compensate them nicely then they will go'.

Donald explained.

'Ok keep your line open with them Tell them I'm still the main speaker and they will be a guest speaker in their field of experty'. Jeff said.

'Now let's discuss about this leasing property thing. Can someone explain to me the whole idea'. Jeff inquired.

'Actually coach it's my idea and I get it from the Money Boot Camp Seminar. I just had a tough why not get a flat with 3 bedrooms then make a profit out of it. Surely, it will help us come up with the amount of money needed. If we can find a flat within the 2 weeks period and we can filled it up with tenants and bed space then our probable income is around 10,000 dirhams minus the rent. But we can first give all the money to our group's fund then we can get the payment from the excess money in the seminar." Donald explained.

'Do you really think this would work?' Jeff asked.

'Well coach you're the one who said that how can we know if we won't try. Besides there's to lose, only we have to issue a checque and a reservation fee of 1,000 dirhams. No down payment or advance. It's really a good deal. – Anna answered.

'Let me tell you one thing – I'm glad about your being open minded and being optimistic. Surely there is a risk in every action or decision that you do, But the greatest risk is not taking risk at all.

Jeff said.

'He continued. I can help you with the checque but you have to come up with the thousand dirhams.

'Guys I'm all in. I'm putting my 200 dirhams in it'. Angie said.

'Let me in. I got an extra 300 here'. – Robert said.

'Let's do it, add this 200'. Donald told everyone.

'Hey don't forget me, my 200 definitely help'. Anna pondered

And now everyone is looking at Jeff…

'Go Coach go!. We just need a hundred! They're all shouting.

'And here's my 100! Jeff put the money on top of the table.

On that moment their team spirit was so high and all of them were very positive.

After the meeting the group went straight to the location of the building they are about to lease.

But at the same time Jeff told them that he has business meeting out of town and will be back soon. For the meantime the group can coordinate to Jeff's executive assistant.

Jeff did not inform the group his contingency plan, For he knew the fact that all odds are against them to gather one hundred thousand dirhams in over a week's time.

So he decided to meet in person his former mentor and business partner who is based in japan. He doesn't want to bring worry or doubt among the team. That's the reason why he did not tell them about it.

He wanted the team on their target to gather that huge amount in over a week time. Nevertheless he left a letter to his receptionist. Just in case they are not going to meet the dead line, he can go to Mr. lee, a business tycoon and his former mentor and business partner as well, to ask for some financial assistance for their One minute Dubai Seminar.

For Mr. lee one hundred thousand dirhams is just a small money. And he can easily finance the seminar and even give them the whole amount they needed for as long as the business plan and the project is profitable.

But one thing is required for him to say yes. Jeff himself should meet him in person. So Jeff did not waste any time. He Immediately contacted Mr. lee and he was told to go and meet him in japan to talk about the deal. On that same day Jeff booked a return ticket to japan.

Its already on the third day since the team has sent the seminar invitation but so far none had reply and worst almost half are inactive or dummy emails.

'Angie do you think we have to revise our invitation? Or should we look for another database of delegates?' Robert asked looking worried.

'I think our database is fine. I'm confident if not today by tomorrow there would be a positive reply. Not to mention the group's circle of network which is close to a thousand people" Angie responded.

'I know we can get hundreds or even thousands of people to sign up. But what I'm afraid of is the time limit we have'. Robert said.

'For as long as we do our part god will take care of the rest'. And the worst case scenario is all of us ending borrowing from bank. I know it's a bad debt but it involves life of a person, in this case it's your son'. Angie told him.

'You're right. We have to leave everything on him. I believe we can come up with that money aside borrowing from bank. Let's keep our hopes up'. Robert said with conviction.

As the afternoon approached, a batch of ladies who work in the same company have inquired about the flat. They were a total of six.

And in the evening on the same day. Another batch of woman went in the flat to check it.

Before the whole day ends a total of 10 people have given their one month advance and each one of them paid six hundred. So the pot money of the group is now six thousand dirhams – just ninety four thousand to go for their target amount.

Come next day, Robert checked his email and phone for any messages but still no one has confirmed

Their interest in the seminar. So he decided to call the team for a general meeting.

They went in the office of Jeff.

"Hi ma'am, good morning! We came here to look for Jeff Gibbons".

Robert said.

"Good morning Robert! Mr. Jeff Gibbons has not come back yet from his out of town business deal.

The receptionist said.

'Do you know when he'll come back? Because it's very urgent. We really need to talk to him'. Angie told the receptionist.

'Well he informed that he would be away for 2 – 3 days'. The receptionist answered.

'I'm trying to reach his mobile but it's going only to his voicemail'.

Do you know where we can contact him'? Robert asked

'Certainly you won't reach his mobile because Mr. Jeff Gibbons is in japan right now. That's where his business deal in. – the receptionist told them.

'What!' but he didn't tell us that he's leaving for japan.' Robert sighed.

The team express their worry upon knowing that Jeff Gibbons had leave the country. Their first thought was he had abandon them in the middle of the crisis.

'Hey guys cheer up! As if he's not coming back. Actually, instructed me to give you this letter just in case you come to look for him'. – the receptionist explained.

The team read the letter all together.

Dear OMD team,

"By the time that you are reading this letter, I have flown and arrived in japan. I'm sorry if I did not inform you ahead about my plan. I decided to go to japan to look for my mentor and my business partner, to finance our seminar project just in case we do not meet the deadline. I'll be back very soon keep up the good work and see you guys back there.

Be bless,
Jeff Gibbons

'So what shall we do now'? Donald said looking worried.

'Nothing changes in the plan. We are still going to wait for the confirmation of the delegates.

Robert answered.

'But Robert it's now the fourth day and we don't have any confirmed delegates yet. Our time is running out.' Angie said

'Everyone just relax okay. I know everything will be alright, and we can get the amount we needed'.

Robert told every one.

'Guys listen, if you will allow me maybe I can speak to my parents and they can help us produce the money'. Anna suggested.

'Anna I really appreciate it, but I don't want to bring more troubles to your family. We can make this happen, right!' Robert addressed them.

'Well I have a suggestion to make'. Donald proposed.

'Go ahead. Tell us what you're thinking.' Robert asked.

'The money that we derived from rental payment can be used to acquire much larger property,

Say a villa, and we can make more profit.' Donald suggested.

'That's a good idea but it's too risky because we only have few more days left. How sure you are that you can get tenants as quickly as we did our first deal?' Anna challenged him.

'Yes true there is a risk involved but there's a big chance we can double or even triple our pot money. And tomorrow is the end of month so I'm sure there will be a lot of people who will look for a new place to stay'. explained Donald.

'How many days you think you can get people to rent in that villa?' Robert asked.

'Well tonight I can work on it give me 2 days and I will let you know if we can get another batch of tenants'. Donald replied.

'Is everyone in favor of Donald's suggestion? Robert asked the team.

Everybody remained silent.

'So it's means all agreed. Okay Donald worked out on it and bring Anna with you. Let me know early in the morning the status.' Robert Told Donald.

The group left Jeff's which is also their HQ.

Donald and Anna went to look for a much bigger place to make a bigger profit from rental property while Robert and Angie continued to look for delegates. They even started calling each individual who replied from the invitation but still no one has confirmed yet.

They all went home very late that day and everyone where tired and exhausted.

Everyone was hopeful that on the 5$^{th}$ day something positive will happen.

It's almost 5 in the morning and it's the 5$^{th}$ day of their mission.

The morning prayer coming from the mosque can be heard all over the city.

Robert woke up and his phone rang.

Ring….ring…. ring….

It's a call back home.

Robert: Hello this is Jeff speaking. Who's this?

Jenny: Robert this is jenny. I'm in the hospital and there is something very important I need to tell you.

Robert: Alright honey I know it's about Joshua's operation. We are working on it, just me few more days.

Jenny: The doctors have said that we need to do the procedure within 24-48 hours because his

Condition is worsening. (sounding tense) and…

Robert: Just relax honey everything will be alright.

Jenny: And the doctors also said that even we do the procedure there is no guarantee 100% that Joshua will recover.

Robert: Let's just put our trust in the lord. just tell the doctors go ahead with the operation and money is not a problem. I love you honey and tell Joshua that I love him so much and we'll play basketball once I go home.

And the line was cut.

Robert: Hello, Hello…

Robert prayed fervently that the lord may give him strength and for his son to become strong in his battle.

He went on his usual exercise routine and meditation in the morning. while he was on the middle of his exercise his phone rang. It's Donald calling him.

'Hey Donald, any updates'? Asked Robert.

'Last night when I went to that villa property I saw in the ads really good. It has a nice facility with garage. Just few blocks away from the Metro. And the good news is, we can double our pot money if we can fill all the rooms with tenants.' explained Donald.

'Okay but what is the catch? Robert wondered

'We have to give all the money we have as a down and security deposit.' Answered Donald.

'So it means giving all what we have right now.' Robert sighed

'And doubling that amount …' Donald replied.

'Do you know that I just got a call from my wife and our son needs to be operated in the next 24-48 hrs. And you want to use all the money that we have'? Robert addressed him

'Bro just trust me on this one. within two days I can get tenants, will double our money and were gonna use it as down for your son's operation'. Donald insisted.

'we have to decide as a team. Let's meet up at the HQ.' Robert Replied

Robert called up the rest of the team for a meeting.

Around twelve in the afternoon the OMD team arrived at Jeff's place to discuss the proposal of Donald to rent out another property and use all their team's fund.

'Guys I really want to thank you for everything. I knew from the beginning of his mission it would really be challenging and it seems impossible to reach for our goal. But I believe that with the right team, Everyone Achieves Miracles.' Robert explained.

'I like that statement bro.' Donald replied

'Thank you. Team, since we started our mission, we've been walking in faith every day in everything that we do. It's on our 5$^{th}$ day today and I know every day is exhausting and pressure day. But back home every day is a gratitude day as my son continues to fight his battle.' Robert said

'That's what we're here for Robert, to fight the battle with your son'. Angie told him.

'Any updates regarding your son? Asked Anna.

'this morning I received a call from my wife and my son needs to be operated within 24-48 hours.' And so far we're still ninety four thousand dirhams short.' Robert said.

'any news from coach? When will he come back?' Angie asked.

'He's secretary told me that Mr. Jeff Gibbons is unreachable since this morning.' Robert answered

'Do we have a contingency plan in absence of him? Anna butt in.

'Actually the whole mission depends on Mr. Jeff Gibbon's even if we gather as many delegates as we can for the seminar, we cannot conduct the seminar without him'. Robert Explained

'And how many confirmed delegates we have?' Donald asked

'Upon checking our database this morning no significant development yet.' Robert Answered

'guys we have to move. We don't know exactly when will coach come back, let alone his whereabouts. We can't afford to lose time while waiting for him.' Donald said

'So what shall we do'? asked Angie

'If the whole team agrees, we will use the team's fund to rent a bigger property then get tenants and we'll double our fund'. Donald explained.

'How sure you are that you can get tenant's within two days? Angie questioned him

'Guys today is the end of the month and a lot of people will be looking for a new place to stay that's I'm sure of.' Donald answered with confidence.'

'And what if we lease the villa and give all our money then we'll have difficulty getting tenants. Remember that we only have barely two days left. Anna said

'Well, the risk that I can see is the delay of making the villa fully occupied. But I don't want to wait for Mr. Jeff Gibbons and do nothing. If you have any better idea then now is the right time to tell it.' Addressed Donald.

Everyday remained silent for few minutes.

Then the secretary of Jeff Gibbons came in the hall where they are meeting.

'Sorry to interrupt you guys but you have to watch this latest news in japan.' The office secretary said

She turned on the cable television inside the meeting hall and everyone where shocked to see the news a major city in Japan was devastated by a strong earthquake then followed by a huge tsunami. And Jeff Gibbons happened to be in that city.

All of them were worried about Jeff's condition.

Robert worried for two things: If Jeff is safe wherever he is; if they can provide the money needed for his sons operation, especially now that his friend and mentor is nowhere to be found.

'Any news from Mr. Gibbons?' I'm sure he's trying to call us. And I'm sure he's safe somewhere else

In Japan.' Robert told the secretary

'Before I entered this room we tried to locate him via GPS but all system in Japan were down.' The secretary explained

'let us pray for his safe journey back here.' Robert said

'So what are we going to do now?' Asked Anna

'Those who are in favor for Donald's idea raise their hand.' Said Robert

Robert raised his hand and the rest followed.

So the group finally decided to put all the money to lease a villa property.

On the same day, they have leased the property and they started to post their ads in the super markets near in the villa. From morning until midnight they didn't take rest. And by midnight they have almost fill up all the rooms, and doubled their pot money.

It's on the $6^{th}$ day of their mission.

At around two o'clock in the morning, Robert received a call from his wife.

> Jenny: Robert do you have the money now?
>
> Robert: I will get it today don't worry.
>
> Jenny: Doctor said our son has to be operated within 24 hours or else his condition will be critical.

Robert: Honey I know that. Tell the go ahead with the operation and we have the money

Jenny: okay. Robert we are counting on you

Robert: may God be with us.

Jenny: I got to go, I'm just using the hospital's facility.

Robert: Alright You take care and our son. I love you

Jenny: love you too

And jenny hang up the phone.

Right at that moment Robert believed and put his trust to God.

'Father in heaven, I know you're up there taking care of everything. Honestly, I'm not sure how we can produce the money we needed but I believe that with you all things are possible. Let thy will be done'. Robert prayed with all his heart.

Then he fell asleep

For the second time he dreamed almost the same vision.

He was holding a young beautiful plant. Little that he knows that young beautiful plant became infected and it died afterwards. What was left is one leaf w/ a branch. Then he tried to put that leaf w/ a branch in a ground soil. He gave it enough water and sunlight, and after sometime it grew and multiplied.

Though he slept very late he still managed to wake up very early in the morning and to do his daily devotion and exercise.

While taking his rest, he received a phone call from on unknown international number.

It was Jeff calling him.

Robert: Hello, this is Robert speaking, who's this?

Jeff: Robert… this is Jeff… (sound is static)

Robert: I can't hear you well who's this again?

Jeff: I said this is Jeff, My line is choppy, you have to bear with me.

Robert: Did you say Jeff. Is this Jeff Gibbons?

Jeff: Yup. This is Jeff. I guess you've watched what happened here. I'm stuck in the city and all the flights are cancelled.

The city where I'm at is severely damaged including their airport so I have to go to the next city to fly back there.

Robert: Thanks God you're fine. We are all worried about you. So when can you fly back here so we can start re-planning our seminar project.

Jeff: My Good news is that my friend agreed to invest in our seminar project and he will finance half of the money we needed.

Robert: Wow! That's a very good news. But coach I have to tell you something… now we got only 1 day left to produce the money because my son needs to be operated within twenty-four hours on his condition will be critical.

Jeff: Sorry to hear that I'll try to fly back as soon as possible. Just hold on to you faith son.

Robert: Yes I am

The line was cut since the telecommunication system was also affected by the calamity.

Their fund doubled because of the tenants they were able to get for the villa they leased.

When they checked their database, only few delegates confirmed their registration.

The agreed to send the money they were able produce. It's total amount is thirteen thousand dirham – still eighty seven thousand dirham short. But before they were able to send the money something happened unexpectedly.

Robert received an sms from Donald.

'Robert we have to talk right now. Tell the group we'll meet up in HQ. in one hour' – Donald

'Donald what is that you want to tell us? Is it good or Bad? Asked Angie

'Guys forgive me. I don't want it to happen. Something went wrong in the villa…' Donald sighed

'What is it Robert? C'mon bro tell us so we can sort it out and solve the problem.' Robert told him

'Guys I regret to inform you that the tenants or our villa wants to get their money back'. Donald told everyone.

'Why? What happened exactly? Anna questioned him.

'the electricity was cut by the Municipality because there are some requirements that did not pass their standard. Also, they imposed some fines and we have to pay for it before they bring back the electricity.' Donald explained.

'So what's the plan now? Now that Donald loose our money for not doing his due due diligence on the property.

'Guys I'm so sorry. I just want our fund to grow. I asked you before if you have better ideas or suggestions while we are waiting for Jeff Gibbons but you all agreed to my proposal right!' Donald defended himself.

'Enough of this! Let's not put the blame on anyone else. It's not going to help the situation. We are all responsible for this and all of us are accountable.' Robert Exclaimed.

'Robert is right. Let's just think and plan for our next move.' Anna suggested

'Donald, how much money are we gonna return? Robert asked

'Half of our fund we have to give them plus the penalty to pay.' Donald answered.

'For the penalty we have to discuss it with the developer' Angie claimed.

'What are we going to do now Robert. We have less than a day to produce the money we needed. I think we have to borrow and whatever is left from our fund we just have to send it now.' Anna said

'Angie isn't it that you have made a fund raising before. You think it's possible to do it again using social networking sites.' Donald told her

'yes I can do that but with time constraint I'm not sure if we can get response as quick as possible.' Angie replied.

'Well let's do it what we have to loose after'? Anna pondered.

'Okay. Let's do it guys! Angie yelled.

'I'm sure coach will be happy to know that we are making things happen while he is away. And by the way, I just talk to him early this morning. He's safe and his trip was successful and he'll be back here as soon as there would be flights available to the next city close to him. Once he's back we can re-focus in our seminar project.' Robert said.

The whole team spent the day until night passing on the message in the social networking sites. They even tapped some groups and community. All of them were hopeful that somehow a miracle will happen.

All of them stayed HQ up until midnight waiting for a big development. In fact they fell asleep inside the meeting room. Probably they have must felt all the pressure, tiredness, they have even skipped most of their meals.

They are on their 7$^{th}$ day of the challenge.

The time is exactly 8 o'clock in the morning. Robert woke up by the ring of his mobile.

Ring…ring…ring…

"hello, who's this?

'I'm calling for Dubai helps and I'm looking for Mr. Robert De La Cruz.'

'Yes, This is Robert speaking how may I help you.'

'I'm calling to tell you sir that you have been selected to be the winner for our yearly medical mission. A lady by the name of Josie have submitted your case to us. I believe that your son is suffering from leukaemia and needs to have a surgery that would cost a hundred thousand dirham. Is that correct sir?'

'yes that's true. In fact the doctor told us we have to perform the procedure as soon as possible. Otherwise, his condition will be critical.'

'We'll you must be a very blessed person because Dubai helps will cover the whole expense of your son's operation. And we need to do this quickly so we can coordinate with the hospital where your is. So please come in our office today.'

'thank you so much madam. If you only knew how much I'm praying for this.'

'We'll this is it. Your prayers have been heard up in heaven.'

'may I know whom I'm speaking with?'

'this is Mercy'

'Your my angel Mercy. Tell everyone in Dubai helps that I'm very grateful and I pray that you may help a lot more people like me.'

'We'll Sir I believe in good karma because when I checked your profile I'm surprise to find out that you have volunteered in one of our mission. So you are just being re-paid for your good deeds. So sir we'll be expecting you to come here as soon as possible.

'Definitely! Thank you! Thank you! Thank you! Be bless Mercy

'Bye.'

'Bye.'

After that conversation Robert shouted for joy and sung praise and worship.

The whole team woke up and when they asked Robert why he became like crazy man, he explained to them the whole phone conversation he had. And everyone celebrated with so much delight and joy.

A lot of things happened along the way, they even reach the point of giving up but they just remained hopeful and positive. They least expected the money where it came from.

That same day the whole team went to the office of Dubai helps to officially receive the award of medical assistance as part of organization's mission.

They have urgently coordinated with the hospital where Robert's son is confined.

They have performed immediately the operation and it was successful.

Jeff Gibbons came back safety after almost two weeks of stay in japan. He has the money they needed originally and they are going to use that for the seminar project.

They agreed to continue the seminar project because after the operation of Robert's son, not only hundreds but thousands of people are very interested to attend the seminar. So it became large scale seminar on life's success. Jeff Gibbons has to expand his operation due to public demand and he made the OMD team his business partners.

All of them has fair share in the series of seminars they have conducted in Dubai.

The OMD team also opened a fund for charity purposes. A portion of their income from the seminars and other business they ventured was donated to medical assistance, education and livelihood

Programs for individuals who would want to go back home to their home country and start a new life.

When all of these things happened right before Robert's eyes he remembered his two dreams before. Now it's clear to him what the message of his vision was.

Robert Decided to stay for another year in Dubai to help and support Jeff Gibbons in his large scale seminar programs. Later on, the seminar programs grew more and it got clients from large organizations and corporations in Dubai and Robert visits Dubai once in a while to become a guest speaker.

Donald and Anna got engaged and they have invested their money in property business, not only in Dubai but globally. They became successful property investors ranging from home individuals to commercial properties.

For Angie she decided to use the money she got from the profit sharing to setup her restaurant business back home. She started with one branch and after a couple of years she branched out another three in different areas.

Once in a while the group meets like every after year or two. And they have started to build their own non-profit organization which aim to help the depressed community and to those people who came back home from abroad and wanted to start a new life.

Robert, Angie, Donald and Anna became successful in all areas of life: career, finance, health, relationship, recreation, helping the community and their spiritual life. Thanks to Jeff Gibbons, because of his mentorship they were no longer corrupted by their success. Furthermore, their story became inspirational to other people who lives and works in Dubai to achieve success and pursue their dreams.

# NE MINUTE Arabic

## Basic Grammar & Common Phrases

| Pronouns | Meanings |
|---|---|
| I | **ana** |
| HE | **hwa** |
| SHE | **hya** |
| IT | **hwa/hya** |
| WE | **nehna** |
| THEY | **homma/henne** |
| YOU (singular) | **enta/enty** |
| YOU (plural) | **ento** |

Where are **you** from?

**enta** mnwein?(singular)

**ento** mn wein? (plural)

GOOD BYE

**Mkkkkkaa el salama,**

**Sharafet/sharafty/s harafto**

Thank You
**shokran**

When addressing someone with respect:

**Hadretak-Hadretek**

| Question | Reply | |
|---|---|---|
| **Alsalam Alaikom** | Peace upon you(hello) | **wa Alaikom alsalam** |
| **Sabah el Khair** | Good Morning | **sabah el noor** |
| **Masaa' el Khair** | Good Evening | **masaa' el noor** |

You're welcome
**Afwan**

I don't speak Arabic

**Ana msh batkalem Arabi**

Do you speak English?

**Enta betekalem**

Speak slowly

**Etkalem shway shway**

| **Masculine** | | **Feminine** |
|---|---|---|
| **Marhaba, keef halak?** | Welcome, How are you? | **Marhaba, keef halek?** |
| --------------------- | Fine/great thank God | --------------------- |
| --------------------- | **bekhair alHamdolah** | --------------------- |
| **Shu aKHbarak?** | What's up? | **Shu aKHbarek** |
| --------------------- | Fine/great thank God | --------------------- |
| --------------------- | **Tamam alHamdolah** | --------------------- |
| **shu esmak?** | What is your name? | **shu esmek?** |
| --------------------- | My name is | --------------------- |
| **Esmaha/esmok** | **esmy** | |
| **momken asAdak?** | How can I help/ assist you? | **Momken asAdek?** |
| --------------------- | I want | --------------------- |
| --------------------- | **baddy/areed** | --------------------- |

IM SORRY!

Masculine: **ana asef**

Feminine: **ana asfa**

**Numbers, Directions & Timelines**

| | | | |
|---|---|---|---|
| 0 = sefer | Sunday = alhad | Today = elyoom | |
| 1 = waHed | Monday = elethnein | Tomorrow = bokra | |
| 2 = etnein | Tuesday = elthalath | The day after tomorrow = baAd bokra | |
| 3 = thalata | Wednesday = elarbaA | Yesterday = embareH/ams | |
| 4 = arbAa | Thursday = elKhamees | Now = alheen/delwa'ty | |
| 5 = KHamsa | Friday = eljomAa | Later = baAd shwaya | |
| 6 = seta | Saturday = elsabt | Next = eljay | |
| 7 = sabaAa | 200 = meteen | 600 =sotomeya | 1000 = ALF |
| 8 = tamanya | 300 = thulthmeya | 700 = SobAomeya | |
| 9 = tesAa | 400 = rubAomeya | 800 = thomnomeya | |
| 10 = Ashara? | 500 = Khumsomeya | 900 = tosAomeya | |

| | | |
|---|---|---|
| Infront= amam | beside = janb | Where? = wein? |
| Straight= Alatool/seeda | go = rooH | elevator = masaAd |
| Left = yassar | up = foa' | washroom =Hammam |
| Right =yameen | go up =etlaA | Prayer room = mussalla |
| Behind =wara | go down = enzel | seats = maqaAed |
| Down = taht | turn = leff | |

# EPILOGUE

The plane where Robert is boarded just landed in his soil country and he was very happy to be back home after five straight years. He was fetched by his wife and his son, who just turned five.

Upon seeing them afar he could not control his emotion and tears started falling from his eyes.

As he embraced them he could not believe that he is now reunited with them. All he can say is thank God for everything he has done into his life. They went straight to their newly purchased brand new dream house and lot.

And his family received a lot of more blessing.

Back in Dubai an airplane carrying passengers who are first timers is about to land at the airport.

And Jeff Gibbons is one of the passengers. He noticed that his seatmate is both excited and fearful, He can tell it in his eyes.

He Approached the gentlemen and talk to him.

Hi! My name is Jeff Gibbons, is this your first time to go here in Dubai? Asked Jeff

Yes sir it's my first time…

# AFTERWORD

Indeed Dubai is a training ground to build your character and it serves as your stepping stone to reach your dreams, aspirations and goals in life.

To be successful is one thing and to be lured and blinded by it is quite another. Truly, working and Living Dubai is one of the greatest opportunities given to me by God.

While writing this book all the personal experiences and encounters I had with different people, coming from different parts of the world, made me conclude: that here in Dubai things will get tougher before it gets easier. And I believe it's also true with other place.

One thing I admire about Dubai is the leadership and how Dubai envisions the future, Dubai welcomes problems as challenges rather than hindrance to its continues development, Let alone the 2008 financial crisis that hit the global economy.

Like Dubai we should also be bold and courageous creating new ideas and facing difficulties in life. And before you know it, things will start to unfold beyond your wildest expectations.

And if you're holding and reading this book now, let me say: Congratulations! You're one step ahead in knowing how to be successful in Dubai whether as expats or tourist alike. Live your dreams and act on it!

<u>ARTHUR JORGE KUIZON</u>

Author

# APPENDIX A

## Interview Highlights

Q1. Why did you choose Dubai?

A. Because Dubai is fantastic, open, great lifestyle. A lot of things to do. It's really safe – Silja fr. Germany.

A. Dubai is still developing and I can be part of the transgression. Unlike in Europe or in other well developed countries where they have reached their peak of growth. – Rjay fr. British Virgin Island

A. Compared to other places, Dubai is very safe place. – Abdulla fr. Kenya

A. Dubai is the perfect place to launch your career. Joe fr. Texas, U.S.A.

Q2. What id your first impression about Dubai?

A. Dubai is an open city. It's leaders are always open for changes and innovation. – Vohid fr. Russia

A. Dubai is a place of haven-tax free, sky is the limit. Dubai is new, fresh, it's like Wild West in the U.S., everybody went to California looking for gold, a lot of people found a lot of people did not. Joe fr. Texas. U.S.A.

A. It's a place where you can see and interact with people from different continents like Asia, Europe, Africa, etc. – Sai fr Myanmar

Q3. How did you adjust with the Multi-Cultural environment in Dubai?

A. I tried to learn other languages through my friend. – Teresia fr. Kenya

A. It is a very interesting experience to live/work with various nationalities. First, I felt irritated or uncomfortable about the cultural differences but now always try to enjoy them. Mina fr. Fukushima, Japan

A. Not much of a problem. With so many Indians, Dubai is the Indian State out of India. – Milton fr. Mumbai, India

A. I humble myself to other nationalities to get their respect. You don't have to be aggressive, you forget about the culture. Narayan fr. Nepal

Q4. What do you like most about Dubai and dislike?

A. I like the warm weather because I'm enable to go beach all year round with my husband. I dislike that people don't follow traffic rules. – Mina fr. Fukushima, Japan

A. What I like most about Dubai is that its ideas, ambitions, and projects are always the best in the world. They always achieve their goals. Vohid fr. Russia

A. I like shopping, fancy restaurant, safety & lifestyle. I dislike careless drivers and doctors. Feruza fr. Uzbekistan

Q5. What is your most unforgettable/best experience in Dubai?

A. When I've heard about happened to my hometown in Japan when my friend and family suffered the earthquake.

I had to still go at work. But my colleagues held a charity for the victims and everybody contributed no matter what the nationality is.

A. When a branded cola drink company paid for my weekly grocery. Feruza fr. Uzbekistan

A. Last 2010 I participated in Dubai Marathon. I did not win but its okay because the money registration will go to an orphanage. Roshan fr. Nepal

A. I just got married but I stayed with my wife for only 2 weeks. I was sad when the plane took off, I was crying. In certain situations there is no choice. Sai fr. Myanmar

A. I got my dream job here in Dubai to be a cabin crew. Teresia fr. Kenya

Q5. How do you spend your free time in Dubai?

A. I go to theme parks, beach parks and Lamcy. These places are close to my heart because I was dating my girlfriend in those places. Amin fr. Pakistan

A. By joining voluntary community works. Daisy fr. U.K.

A. Capturing shots of great locations and events. Robin fr. U.K.

A. Go to beach with my husband and go for body boarding and spending time in bookstore and reading my favorite Japanese books. Mina fr. Fukushima Japan

A. Attending different events with different people and spending time in the mall seeing beautiful women. Vohid fr. Russia

Q6. How long do you plan to stay in Dubai?

A. I will stay until I find my next purpose in life. Mina fr. Fukushima, Japan

A. If you're not an Emirati, Dubai is only a passing cloud. You will not be here forever. After I have save enough I am ready to go back home. Teresia fr. Kenya

A. For as long as my business is up and running. Feruza fr. Uzbekistan

A. Maybe 5 years I'm getting old and I miss my home country. Nothing beats home. Bilal fr. Kenya

Q7. Would you recommend Dubai to your friend and family?

A. Yes. Because it gives you an opportunity to achieve your goals. Feruza fr. Uzbekistan

A. Surely. Dubai is a great place to live. Kavoos fr. Iran

Q8. What is your message to the people out there who would want to go to Dubai?

A. Dubai will make you strong as a person. Abdurahim fr. East Africa

A. The reason were here is adventure and curiosity about the world. It's important to nurture that. You have to learn things – be creative, enjoy your life, enjor your living if not, be home live with your family because that's important too. We all make sacrifices – make sure you're saving, learning, growing, if you're doing that, then carry on. Joe fr. Texas, U.S.A

# Appendix B

## Emergency Phone Numbers

Police: 999

Fire Department: 997

Electricity: 991

Water: 991

Dubai Flights

Dubai International Airport: 04- 224-5555

Dubai Airport Flight Information Voice Portal: 04- 216 6666

Flight Enquiry: 04-224-5777

Emirates: 04-2144444

Directory Enquiry & Yellow Pages in English & Arabic: 181

Al Ameen service from Dubai Police(To report criminal activity or if someone is harassing you): 800-4-888

Amer Service, Dubai Naturalization and Residency Department Hotline: 8005111

Dubai Municipality Public Health Department (For consumer-safety complaints): 04-2232323

UAE Central Bank Control & Inspection(For customer complaints against banks): 04-3939777

Labour complaints toll-free hotline: 800 665

Unified Labour Complaint (For labour and work related complaints): 04-3139900

**Dubai Hospitals**

Al Maktoum Hospital:04 228-4584

Al Wasl Hospital: 04 219-3000

Baraha Hospital: 04 271-0000

Rashid Hospital: 04 337-1323

Welcare Hospital: 04 282-9900

AmericanHospital (336 7777; Oud Metha, Bur Dubai) This private hospital has an excellent 24-hour emergency department and clinic. 04 309-6645

DubaiLondonClinic(344 6663; Al-Wasl Rd, Jumeirah) A private medical centre that also has an emergency department.

NewDubaiHospital (222 9171; Abu Baker al- Siddiq Rd & Al-Khaleej Rd, Hor al-Anz) A government hospital with a decent 24-hour emergency department. 04 219-5000

Sondos Pharmacy (346 0660; Al- Dhiyafah Rd, Satwa) A 24-hour pharmacy that will deliver.

## Telecommunications

Telecommunications are excellent, both within the UAE and with the outside world. There are two service providers Etisalat & Du.

Telephone calls within Dubai city are free. Direct dialling is available to most countries.

To complain about Etisalat's mobile coverage or quality of service: 800 1111050

To complain about Du's mobile coverage or quality of service: 800 1122333

Credit Card Complaints

Mastercard International: 04- 3914200

Visa International : 04- 3319690

American Express : 800- 4931

Diner's Club: 04- 3495800

Dubai Weather Forecast (from Dubai Meteorological Office at Dubai Airport): 04-2162218

# APPENDIX C

## Consulates in Dubai

**American General Consulate**
Telephone: +971 4 3116000
Fax: +971 4 3318594
WebSite: www.usembabu.gov.ae

**Australian General Consulate**
Telephone: +971 4 3212444
Fax: +971 4 3212677
WebSite: www.austrade.gov.au

**Bangladesh Republic Consulate General**
Telephone: +971 4 2726966
Fax: +971 4 2727965

**British General Consulate**
Telephone: +971 4 3971070
Fax: +971 4 3094301
WebSite: www.britain-uae.org

**Canadian Consulate**
Telephone: +971 4 3145555
Fax: +971 4 3145557
WebSite: http://www.canada.org

**Consulate Of Denmark**
Telephone: +971 4 2227699
Fax: +971 4 2235751

**Consulate Of Libya**
Telephone: +971 4 3973972
Fax: +971 4 3970092

**Consulate Of Philippine**
Telephone: +971 4 2667745
Fax: +971 4 2688665

**Consulate Of Russia**
Telephone: +971 4 2231272
Fax: +971 4 2231585

**Consulate Of Singapore**
Telephone: +971 4 3353770
Fax: +971 4 3353771

**Consulate Of Somalia Democratic Republic**
Telephone: +971 4 2958282
Fax: +971 4 2957570

**Consulate Of Sri Lanka**
Telephone: +971 4 3986535
Fax: +971 4 3984687
WebSite: www.srilankaconsul.org.ae

**Consulate Of Switzerland**
Telephone: +971 4 3290999
Fax: +971 4 3313679

**France Consulate General**
Telephone: +971 4 3329040
Fax: +971 4 3328033
WebSite: www.consunatfrance.ae

**German Union Republic Consulate General**

Telephone: +971 4 3972333
Fax: +971 4 3972225
WebSite: www.germanconsulatedubai.org.ae

**Indian Consulate General**

Telephone: +971 4 3971333
Fax: +971 4 3970453
WebSite: www.cgidubai.com

**Indonasian Republic Consulate General**

Telephone: +971 4 3985666
Fax: +971 4 3980804
WebSite:

**Iranian Islamic Republic Consulate General**

Telephone: +971 4 3444717
Fax: +971 4 3449499
WebSite: www.iranconsul.org.ae

**Iraq Consulate General**

Telephone: +971 4 2685445
Fax: +971 4 2625242

**Italian Consulate General**

Telephone: +971 4 3314167
Fax: +971 4 3317469
WebSite: www.italian-embassy.org.ae

**Japan Consulate General**

Telephone: +971 4 3319191
Fax: +971 4 3319292

**Jordan Hashimith Kingdom Consulate General**

Telephone: +971 4 3970500
Fax: +971 4 3971675

**Kingdom Of Holland Consulate**
Telephone: +971 4 3528700
Fax: +971 4 3510502

**Kingdom Of Norway Consulate**
Telephone: +971 4 3533833
Fax: +971 4 3533915

**Kingdom Of Thailand Consulate General**
Telephone: +971 4 3492863
Fax: +971 4 3490932

**Kuwait General Consulate**
Telephone: +971 4 3978000
Fax: +971 4 3977707

**Lebanese Consulate General**
Telephone: +971 4 3977450
Fax: +971 4 3977431
WebSite: www.lebsoncd.org

**Malaysia Consulate General**
Telephone: +971 4 3355538
Fax: +971 4 3352220
WebSite: www.matrade.gov.my

**Newzealand Consulate General**
Telephone: +971 4 3317500
Fax: +971 4 3317501
WebSite: www.nzte.govt.nz

**Ozbekistan Republic Consulate General**
Telephone: +971 4 3947400
Fax: +971 4 3945234

**Pakistan Consulate General**
Telephone: +971 4 3970412
Fax: +971 4 3971975

**Palestine Consulate General**
Telephone: +971 4 3972020
Fax: +971 4 3972373

**Qatar Consulate General**
Telephone: +971 4 3982888
Fax: +971 4 3983555

**Republic Of China Consulate General**
Telephone: +971 4 3944733
Fax: +971 4 3952207

**Republic Of Egypt Consulate General**
Telephone: +971 4 3971122
Fax: +971 4 3971033

**Romanian Consulate General**
Telephone: +971 4 3940580
Fax: +971 4 3940992

**Saudi Arabia Kingdom Consulate General**
Telephone: +971 4 3979777
Fax: +971 4 3979614

**South Africa Consulate**
Telephone: +971 4 3975222
Fax: +971 4 3979602
WebSite: www.southafrica.ae

**Sudan Republic Consulate General**
Telephone: +971 4 2637555
Fax: +971 4 2637080

**Swedish Consulate General**
Telephone: +971 4 3457716
Fax: +971 4 3452439
WebSite: www.swedchamb.com

**Syrian Arab Republic Consulate General**
Telephone: +971 4 2663354
Fax: +971 4 2653393

**Tunisian Republic Consulate**
Telephone: +971 4 2277270
Fax: +971 4 2277667

**Turkish General Consulate**
Telephone: +971 4 3314788
Fax: +971 4 3317317

**Vietnam Consulate General**
Telephone: +971 4 3988924
Fax: +971 4 3988624

**Yemen Arab Republic Consulate General**
Telephone: +971 4 3970131
Fax: +971 4 3972901

# Appendix D

**Dubai Business Climate - it offers the best of all worlds from travel to leisure to networking and business opportunities.**

In the UAE, economic activity is regulated by individual emirates as well as the Federal Government. In Dubai, the authorities have deliberately sought to create an environment which is well ordered without being unduly restrictive. As a result, Dubai offers businessmen operating conditions that are among the most liberal and attractive in the region.

There are many options open to international companies seeking to establish a business relationship with Dubai. Apart from forming a trading relationship, many companies find that there are distinct advantages in having an on-the-spot presence in order to research market prospects, make contacts, liaise with customers, and see through the details of any transactions and orders secured.

Having such a presence can provide considerable business advantages in the Middle East. Businessmen in the region prefer to deal with someone they know and trust and personal relationships are much more important in doing business in the Arab world than they are in western Europe or America. Also, the buying patterns of some countries served by Dubai tend to be unpredictable, creating a need for first class market intelligence and information.

Read more: http://www.dubaitourism.ae/WorkingWithDubai/SettingUp/tabid/85/language/en-US/Default.aspx#ixzz1Dq5Ju3Nq

Licensing

The basic requirement for all business activity in Dubai is one of the following three categories of licences:

1. Commercial licences covering all kinds of trading activity;
2. Professional licences covering professions, services, craftsmen and artisans;
3. Industrial licences for establishing industrial or manufacturing activity.

These licences are issued by the Dubai Economic Development Department (with the exception of licences for hotels and other tourism-related businesses which are issued by the Department of Tourism and Commerce Marketing.) Also, licences for some categories of business require approval from certain ministries and other authorities: for example, banks and financial institutions from the Central Bank of the UAE; insurance companies and related agencies from the Ministry of Economy and Commerce; manufacturing from the Ministry of Finance and Industry; and pharmaceutical and medical products from the Ministry of Health.

More detailed procedures apply to businesses engaged in oil or gas production and related industries.

In general, all commercial and industrial businesses in Dubai should be registered with the Dubai Chamber of Commerce and Industry.

Read more: http://www.dubaitourism.ae/WorkingWithDubai/SettingUp/tabid/85/language/en-US/Default.aspx#ixzz1Dq5eAT3A

Ownership Requirements

Fifty-one per cent participation by UAE nationals is the general requirement for all UAE established companies except:

- Where the law requires 100% local ownership;
- In the Jebel Ali and Airport Free Zones;
- In activities open to 100% AGCC ownership;
- Where wholly owned AGCC companies enter into partnership with UAE nationals;
- In respect of foreign companies registering branches or a representative office in Dubai;
- In professional or artisan companies where 100% foreign ownership is permitted.
- Read more: http://www.dubaitourism.ae/WorkingWithDubai/SettingUp/tabid/85/language/en-US/Default.aspx#ixzz1Dq61tk4Z

**Legal structures for Business**

Federal Law No. 8 of 1984, as amended by Federal Law No. 13 of 1988 - the Commercial Companies Law - and its by-laws govern the operations of foreign business. In broad terms the provisions of these regulations are as follows:

The Federal Law stipulates a total local equity of not less than 51% in any commercial company and defines seven categories of business organisation which can be established in the UAE. It sets out the requirements in terms of shareholders, directors, minimum capital levels and incorporation procedures. It further lays down provisions governing conversion, merger and dissolution of companies. The seven categories of business organisation defined by the Law are:

- General partnership company
- Partnership-en-commendam
- Joint venture company
- Public shareholding company
- Private shareholding company
- Limited liability company
- Share partnership company

## Partnerships

General partnership companies are limited to UAE nationals only. The Dubai government does not presently encourage the establishment of partnership-en-commendam and share partnership companies.

## Joint Venture Companies

A joint venture is a contractual agreement between a foreign party and a local party licensed to engage in the desired activity. The local equity participation in the joint venture must be at least 51%, but the profit and loss distribution can be prescribed. There is no need to license the joint venture or publish the agreement. The foreign partner deals with third parties under the name of the local partner who (unless the agreement is publicised) bears all liability.

In practice, joint ventures are seen as offering a suitable structure for companies working together on specific projects.

## Public and Private Shareholding Companies

The Law stipulates that companies engaging in banking, insurance, or financial activities should be run as public shareholding companies. Foreign banks, insurance and financial companies, however, can establish a presence in Dubai by opening a branch or representative office.

Shareholding companies are suitable primarily for large projects or operations, since the minimum capital required is Dh. 10 million (US$ 2.725 million) for a public company, and Dh. 2 million (US$ 0.545 million) for a private shareholding company. The chairman and majority of directors must be UAE nationals and there is less flexibility of profit distribution than is permissible in the case of limited liability companies.

## Limited Liability Companies

A limited liability company can be formed by a minimum of two and a maximum of 50 persons whose liability is limited to their shares in the company's capital. Such companies are recognised as offering a suitable structure for organisations interested in developing a long term relationship in the local market.

In Dubai, the minimum capital is currently Dh. 300,000 (US$ 82,000), contributed in cash or in kind. While foreign equity in the company may not exceed 49%, profit and loss distribution can be prescribed. Responsibility for the management of a limited liability company can be vested in the foreor national partners or a third party.

The following steps are required in establishing a limited liability company in Dubai.

- Select a commercial name for the company and have it approved by the Licensing Department of the Economic Development Department;
- Draw up the company's Memorandum of Association and have it notarised by a Notary Public in the Dubai Courts;
- Seek approval from the Economic Development Department and apply for entry in the Commercial Register;

- Once approval is granted, the company will be entered in the Commercial Register and have its Memorandum of Association published in the Ministry of Economy and Commerce's Bulletin. The licence will then be issued by the Economic Development Department;
- The company should then be registered with the Dubai Chamber of Commerce and Industry.

**Branches and Representative Offices of Foreign Companies**

The Commercial Companies Law covers the formation and regulation of branches and representative offices of foreign companies in the UAE and stipulates that they may be 100% foreign owned, provided a local agent is appointed.

Only UAE nationals or companies 100% owned by UAE nationals may be appointed as local agents (which should not be confused with the term commercial agent). Local agents - also often referred to as sponsors - are not involved in the operations of the company but assist in obtaining visas, labour cards, etc and are paid a lump sum and/or a percentage of profits or turnover.

Read more: http://www.dubaitourism.ae/WorkingWithDubai/Setting Up/tabid/85/language/en-US/Default.aspx#ixzz1Dq6Eurvh

To establish a branch or representative office in Dubai, a foreign company should proceed as follows:

- Apply for a licence from the Ministry of Economy and Commerce, submitting an agency agreement with a UAE national or 100% UAE owned company. Before issuing the licence, the Ministry will:
- forward the application to the Economic Development Department to obtain the approval of the Dubai government;

- forward the application specifying the activity that the office or branch will be authorised to undertake in the UAE, to the Federal Foreign Companies Committee for approval;
- Once this has been done, the Ministry of Economy and Commerce will issue the required Ministerial licence specifying the activity to be practised by the foreign company;
- The branch or office should be entered in the Economic Development Department's Commercial Register, and the required licence will be issued;
- The branch or office should also be entered in the Foreign Companies Register of the Ministry of Economy and Commerce;
- Finally, the branch or office should be registered with the Dubai Chamber of Commerce and Industry.

Readmore: http://www.dubaitourism.ae/WorkingWithDubai/Setting Up/tabid/85/language/en-US/Default.aspx#ixzz1Dq6X3kWa

Professional firms

In setting up a professional firm, 100% foreign ownership, sole proprietorships or civil companies are permitted. Such firms may engage in professional or artisan activities but the number of staff members that may be employed is limited. A UAE national must be appointed as local service agent, but he has no direct involvement in the business and is paid a lump sum and/or percentage of profits or turnover. The role of the local service agent is to assist in obtaining licences, visas, labour cards, etc.

Read more: http://www.dubaitourism.ae/WorkingWithDubai/Setting Up/tabid/85/language/en-US/Default.aspx#ixzz1Dq75w81o